*The Truth of Suffering
and the Path of Liberation*

SELECTED TITLES
BY CHÖGYAM TRUNGPA

Cutting Through Spiritual Materialism
Meditation in Action
The Myth of Freedom and the Way of Meditation
Ocean of Dharma
The Pocket Chögyam Trungpa
The Sanity We Are Born With
Shambhala: The Sacred Path of the Warrior
Training the Mind and Cultivating Loving-Kindness

The Truth *of* Suffering

and the
Path of Liberation

CHÖGYAM TRUNGPA

Compiled and edited by Judith L. Lief

SHAMBHALA
BOSTON & LONDON
2009

Shambhala Publications, Inc.
Horticultural Hall
300 Massachusetts Avenue
Boston, Massachusetts 02115
www.shambhala.com

9 8 7 6 5 4 3 2 1

First edition
Printed in the United States of America
◎This edition is printed on acid-free paper that meets the
American National Standards Institute z39.48 Standard.
♻This book was printed on 30% postconsumer recycled paper.
For more information please visit us at www.shambhala.com.

Distributed in the United States by Random House, Inc., and
in Canada by Random House of Canada Ltd

Designed by Margery Cantor

Library of Congress Cataloging-in-Publication Data
Trungpa, Chögyam, 1939–1987.
The truth of suffering and the path of liberation / Chögyam Trungpa;
edited by Judith L. Lief.
p. cm.
Includes bibliographical references and index.
ISBN 978-1-59030-668-0 (hardcover: alk. paper)
1. Four Noble Truths. 2. Suffering—Religious aspects—Buddhism.
3. Buddhism—Doctrines. I. Lief, Judith L. II. Title.
BQ4230.T78 2009
294.3'42—dc22
2008037825

CONTENTS

Editor's Preface   vii

Editor's Acknowledgments   xiii

The First Turning of the Wheel of Dharma   xv

Introduction   1

THE FIRST NOBLE TRUTH
   The Truth of Suffering
   1. Recognizing the Reality of Suffering   7
   2. Dissecting the Experience of Suffering   13

THE SECOND NOBLE TRUTH
   The Truth of the Origin of Suffering
   3. The Power of Flickering Thoughts   33
   4. The Development of Set Patterns   39
   5. Perpetually Re-creating Suffering   45

THE THIRD NOBLE TRUTH
   The Truth of Cessation
   6. Awakening and Blossoming   63
   7. Meditation as the Path to Buddhahood   69
   8. Transcending Samsara and Nirvana   75

THE FOURTH NOBLE TRUTH

The Truth of the Path

9. The Doubtless Path   91

10. The Five Paths   97

The Practice of Meditation   117

Outline of Teachings   119

Notes   127

Glossary   131

Text Sources   141

Resources   143

Index   145

EDITOR'S PREFACE

IN THIS BOOK, Chögyam Trungpa discusses the Buddhist teachings on the four noble truths with great clarity and insight. He takes these seemingly simple teachings and systematically uncovers many layers of subtlety and sophistication. His presentation skillfully weaves together a scholarly exposition of the material with a fresh and up-to-date interpretation geared toward the contemporary dharma practitioner. Like a great jazz musician, Trungpa focuses on a central theme, explores it in depth, and then takes off into magnificent riffs of improvisation before returning once again to core principles. As is typical of his teaching, he repeatedly connects the material he is discussing with the meditative and contemplative practices that bring such teachings to life.

Chögyam Trungpa Rinpoche (1940–1987) was formally trained in the Tibetan monastic tradition, as the eleventh Trungpa Tülku and abbot of Surmang Monastery in eastern Tibet. (*Rinpoche* is a Tibetan honorific meaning "Precious One" or "Precious Jewel." The term *tülku* indicates a person who is considered to be a reincarnation or spiritual heir of a specific teacher.) Like many other Tibetans, he fled his country after the Communist takeover and entered India as a refugee. From India, he traveled to Great Britain, where he studied Western arts and culture at Oxford University, before moving to North America in 1970. Trungpa Rinpoche was one of the first Tibetan lamas to arrive in the United States and Canada, and he became a pivotal figure in introducing Tibetan Buddhism to Western students.

Chögyam Trungpa Rinpoche was an innovative spiritual leader, continually experimenting with new forms of transmitting the dharma that would allow it to take root in modern Western society not as an alien or exotic novelty but as a genuine living tradition. He did not fall back on familiar pedagogical approaches more suited for Tibetan monastics, nor did he present the dharma in the dry language of the academy. Instead he brought the teachings to life, speaking directly with no exoticism or cultural trappings—and in English! This was a radical and controversial approach.

Trungpa Rinpoche had an uncanny ability to communicate in a way that each student thought he was talking directly to him or her alone. He was able to connect the teachings with the day-to-day experiences of ordinary people, and show a way for laypeople to join their lives with practice and study as "householder yogis." At the same time, his exposition was true to the depth and profundity of his tradition. Although he taught in the West for only seventeen years (from 1970 to 1987), his influence has been immense and continues to unfold.

The four noble truths are central to the Buddhist tradition. The Buddha presented these core teachings in one of the first sermons he gave after his enlightenment, and they were recorded in the sutra entitled "The First Turning of the Wheel of Dharma." (An excerpt from this sutra appears on page xv.) In later teachings the Buddha touched on the four noble truths repeatedly, expanding upon and further elucidating his original presentation. In this volume, Trungpa Rinpoche approaches the four noble truths from the practitioner's perspective, joining a discussion of the view, or intellectual understanding of these teachings, with a discussion of the application, or how that view might be realized in practice.

Trungpa Rinpoche stresses the importance of recognizing how entrenched we are in habitual patterns of suffering. Although we might prefer to muse about happiness and how we can get more of it, it is our blind stumbling after happiness that has entrapped us in the first place. The first truth, the truth of suffering, lays it on the line: suffering is real, and it cannot be avoided. For the practitioner, the starting point is taking a cold, hard look at our situation, honestly and dispassionately. It is essential to break our long-standing habit of avoidance and wishful thinking.

Once we have overcome our resistance to facing the fact of suffering, we have the opportunity to examine its cause. According to the second noble truth, the cause of suffering is fundamental ignorance and desire. Trungpa Rinpoche discusses this truth in terms of subtle shifts of thought turning into fixations, then into emotions such as jealousy or hatred, and finally into actions. The value of meditation practice is that the practitioner learns to notice this pattern at an early stage, and is thus able to catch these subtle shifts of thought before they escalate into harmful actions with their inevitable repercussions.

One could say that the first two truths are a reality check, allowing us to begin on solid footing. The reason it is possible for us to look at our experience in such a way is that we begin to develop a sense of contrast in the form of the third noble truth, the truth of cessation. We realize that it is possible to free ourselves from suffering. Having understood both how suffering arises and how we perpetuate it, we can liberate ourselves not only from the consequences of suffering, but also from the underlying cause.

Without glimpsing the possibility of cessation, it would be very difficult to stick with the practice. The notion of enlightenment, or liberation from suffering, would seem to be only a remote possibility. But even ordinary practitioners experience gaps in the cycle of suffering. We all experience signs of awakening and transformation, if only briefly, or from time to time. According to Trungpa Rinpoche, while we should not seek out such signs of progress, it is important to appreciate such experiences and use them to develop greater confidence and trust in ourselves and in the dharma.

Having been given a hint of what is possible, we are inspired to do what it takes to get there. Thus, the fourth noble truth is the truth of the path. From the time of the Buddha, many guidelines have developed to help the student on the journey to enlightenment. At the same time, each student must forge his or her own way. Although effort is required, realization cannot be produced. Realization is inherent within the path itself. In following the path, confusion is overcome and wisdom dawns as surely and naturally as the sun rises in the east.

This volume is derived from talks given at three-month training programs called Vajradhatu Seminaries, a series of annual retreats Trungpa Rinpoche offered to his closest students. Trungpa Rinpoche developed the Seminary format to give his senior students a detailed map of the Buddhist path and to steep them in meditation practice. Intensive group meditation practice created the proper container for such teachings to take root, not as abstract theory, but in the form of practical guidelines for the meditation practitioner. Having introduced his core teachings in this way, Trungpa Rinpoche also expressed the desire to offer these teachings to the broader world when the time was ripe.

Following Tibetan tradition, Trungpa Rinpoche structured Seminaries according to three progressive stages of practice and realization: the hinayana, or "lesser vehicle," the mahayana, or "greater vehicle," and the vajrayana, or "indestructible vehicle." The hinayana refers to the path of individual development, exemplified by the *arhat;* the mahayana refers to the joining of wisdom and compassionate action, exemplified by the *bodhisattva;* and the vajrayana refers to the path of fearless engagement and spiritual daring, exemplified by the *siddha.* The literal translation of hinayana as "lesser vehicle" may give the impression that it is unsophisticated or inferior. However, according to Tibetan Buddhist tradition, the hinayana provides the foundation for the entire path. In the three-yana journey, each yana, or vehicle, is rooted in an understanding of the previous one. So the hinayana is not left behind as a student progresses to the mahayana and vajrayana, but it continues. The yanas are like a series of concentric circles, with each larger circle fully encompassing what came before. The three yanas build upon one another, continually strengthening, expanding upon, and enriching each other. The four noble truths are the foundation of the hinayana, and of the entire Buddhist path.

Traditional presentations of the four noble truths, as well as other central Buddhist teachings, are filled with lists, terms, and detailed outlines, which can make for dry reading. At the same time, such outlines can serve as invaluable references and study aids. (As an example, see "Outline of Teachings," page 119. In his presentation of the four noble truths, Trungpa Rinpoche provides a link between such traditional presentations of the teachings and our own experience of the path. He introduces the possibility of uncovering progressively subtler insights into the nature of mind and experience and gives us the tools to be able to communicate those insights to others.

In his presentation of the four noble truths Chögyam Trungpa frequently refers to the teaching of Jamgön Kongtrül (1813–1900), a renowned Tibetan Buddhist master, scholar, writer, and the founder of the Ri-me, or nonsectarian, movement. Jamgön Kongtrül authored more than one hundred volumes, of which the most well known are his *Five Treasuries,* comprehensive works spanning the entire range of Tibetan Buddhism. Like many Tibetan teachers, Trungpa Rinpoche carried with him a compact edition of this monumental work and consulted it again and again.

The teachings of the four noble truths are both ancient and up-to-date. They have been handed down from teacher to student for centuries, yet they apply to our own immediate experience. In each moment, the pattern of the four truths repeats itself: the truth of suffering and the origin of suffering, and the truth of freedom from suffering and the path to liberation. Therefore, in each moment we have a choice: we can continue to perpetuate our suffering, or we can interrupt that pattern at its source and attain a glimpse of liberation.

The teachings of the four noble truths are grounded in our ordinary experiences as human beings. It is by relating with these experiences, rather than by escaping them, that we can free ourselves. The radical message of the Buddha is that the potential for freedom is always at hand, and it is up to us—no one else—what we do with that.

May the teachings of the four noble truths be of benefit to all suffering beings who long for liberation. May the legacy of Chögyam Trungpa Rinpoche continue to unfold, illuminating the way of the Buddha, the path of meditation, and the power of Buddhist practice and understanding to address the challenges of daily life in contemporary society.

—Judith L. Lief

EDITOR'S ACKNOWLEDGMENTS

I WOULD LIKE TO acknowledge the many students whose efforts have made possible the creation of this handbook on the four noble truths. Countless people have been involved in the recording, transcribing, preserving, editing, and production of these precious teachings. These dedicated students worked anonymously, steadily, and humbly at the many other tasks, essential to this work, purely out of their own inspiration and devotion.

Carolyn Rose Gimian offered her ongoing insightful advice and support. Ellen Kearney provided invaluable help throughout the editing process, working extremely closely with me in a series of editorial retreats, applying her copyediting skills and offering excellent feedback. Thank you to Ben Moore, director of Vajradhatu Publications, for his enthusiastic support. Gordon Kidd, Helen Bonzi, and the staff of Shambhala Recordings and the Shambhala Archives provided needed source materials. Many thanks to John Rockwell for providing valuable feedback and, in particular, for his informal translations of key sections of *The Treasury of Knowledge*. Special thanks to Scott Wellenbach of the Nālandā Translation Committee, who carefully reviewed the technical terminology and helped resolve many challenging editorial issues. Many thanks to Eden Steinberg of Shambhala Publications for her insightful feedback. Lady Diana Mukpo graciously gave her blessing and encouragement to this project. Samuel Bercholz, founder of Shambhala Publications, has been a consistent catalyst in moving the root-text project forward.

Endeavors such as this one require the generous support of donors. We are grateful for the support of the Shambhala Trust and for the anonymous donations we received to help us with this valuable work.

Most especially we would like to acknowledge the Vidya-dhara, Chögyam Trungpa Rinpoche, who in his seventeen years in North America generously and steadfastly dedicated himself to bringing true dharma to the Western world. May the teachings and practices he so carefully introduced be studied, practiced, realized, and carried forth for future generations. May they benefit countless beings and free those who suffer cruelly and needlessly. May we cultivate wisdom, compassion, and the skill to manifest them in action.

The First Turning of the Wheel of Dharma

It is said that after his enlightenment, the Buddha gave his first teachings at Deer Park in what is now known as Sarnath, near Varanasi, India. It was there that he first presented the noble eightfold path and the four noble truths. This is referred to as the first turning of the wheel of dharma.

BROTHERS, THERE ARE FOUR TRUTHS: the existence of suffering, the cause of suffering, the cessation of suffering, and the path which leads to the cessation of suffering. I call these the Four Noble Truths. The first is the existence of suffering. Birth, old age, sickness, and death are suffering. Sadness, anger, jealousy, worry, anxiety, fear, and despair are suffering. Separation from loved ones is suffering. Association with those you hate is suffering. Desire, attachment, and clinging to the five aggregates are suffering.

Brothers, the second truth is the cause of suffering. Because of ignorance, people cannot see the truth about life, and they become caught in the flames of desire, anger, jealousy, grief, worry, fear, and despair.

Brothers, the third truth is the cessation of suffering. Understanding the truth of life brings about the cessation of every grief and sorrow and gives rise to peace and joy.

Brothers, the fourth truth is the path which leads to the cessation of suffering. It is the Noble Eightfold Path, which I have

Excerpted from *Old Path White Clouds* by Thich Nhat Hanh

just explained. The Noble Eightfold Path is nourished by living mindfully. Mindfulness leads to concentration and understanding which liberates you from every pain and sorrow and leads to peace and joy. I will guide you along this path of realization.

*The Truth of Suffering
and the Path of Liberation*

Introduction

WE ARE BORN as human beings, as we are quite aware, and we have to maintain ourselves and keep up our humanness. We do this by breathing, so that our body has the proper circulation and pulsations it needs to survive. We do it by eating food as fuel and by wearing clothes to protect ourselves from the weather. But we can't maintain ourselves in those ways alone, just by eating, wearing clothes, and sleeping so that we can wake up with the daylight and collect more food to eat. There is something else happening beyond that level: emotionally, we feel that we need to accept and reject.

Sometimes we feel very lonely, and sometimes we feel claustrophobic. When we feel lonely, we seek out partners, friends, and lovers. But when we have too many, we become claustrophobic and reject some of them. Sometimes we feel good. Everything has developed ideally for us. We have companionship; we have clothing to keep ourselves warm; we have food in our stomach; we have enough liquid to drink to keep from being thirsty. We feel satisfied. But any one of those satisfactions can subside. We might have companionship but not a good meal; we might have a good meal but no companionship. Sometimes we have good food, but we are thirsty. Sometimes we are happy about one thing but unhappy about other things. It is very hard to keep together the myriad things that go on and on, up and down. It is very hard. It turns out to be quite a handful, quite a project, for us to keep everything at the ideal level. It is almost impossible to maintain an even sense of happiness.

Even though some of our requirements might be achieved, we still feel anxiety. We think, "At this point my stomach is full of food, but where am I going to get my next meal when my stomach is empty and I'm hungry? At this point, I'm all right, but the next time I become thirsty, where am I going to get a drop of water? Right now, I'm fully clothed and I feel comfortable, but just in case it gets hot or cold, what will I do? I'm completely well equipped with companions now, but in case they don't keep me company, where will I find more companionship? What if the person who is presently keeping company with me decides to leave me?"

There are all sorts of jigsaw puzzles in life, and the pieces do not perfectly meet. Even if they did meet—which is highly improbable, one chance in a million or less—you would still be anxious, thinking, "Supposing something goes wrong, then what?" So when you are at your best and you feel good about things, you are even more anxious, because you may not have continuity. And often, you feel cheated by your life, because you do not have the facility to synchronize thousands of things at once. So there is natural, automatic pain and suffering. It is not like the pain of a headache or the pain you feel when some-body hits you in the ribs—it is anxiousness, which is a very haunting situation.

People might say, "I have everything sorted out, and I'm quite happy the way I am. I don't have to look for something to make myself more comfortable." Nonetheless, people are always anxiety-ridden. Apart from simply functioning, the way we gaze at the wall or the mountains or the sky, the way we scratch, the way we timidly smile, the way we twitch our faces, the way we move unnecessarily—the way we do everything—is a sign of anxiousness. The conclusion is that everybody is neurotic, that neurosis creates discomfort and anxiety, and that basic anxiety is happening all the time.

In order to rectify that basic anxiousness, we create heavy-handed situations. We come up with intense aggression; we come up with intense passion; we come up with intense pride. We come up with what are known as the *kleshas*—conflicting or confused emotions—which entertain our basic anxiety and exaggerate it altogether. We do all sorts of things because of that basic anxiety, and because of that, we begin to find ourselves in more trouble and more pain. As the afterthought of expressing our aggression and lust, we find ourselves feeling bad; and not only do we feel bad, but we feel more anxious. That pattern happens all the time. We are in a state of anxiety, and each time we try to make ourselves feel better, we feel worse. We might feel better at the time, if we strike out with our particular flair or style; but then there is a tremendous letdown and tremendous pain. We feel funny about it; in fact, we feel wretched. Not only that, but we make other people feel wretched as well. We can't just practice passion, aggression, and ignorance on ourselves alone; we do it to somebody else as well, and someone always gets hurt. So, instead of just having our own anxiety, we produce a further state of anxiety in others. We generate their anxiety, and they also generate it themselves; and we end up with what is known as "the vicious circle of samsara." Everybody is constantly making everybody else feel bad.

We have been participating in this tremendous project, this constant mishap, this terribly bad mistake, for a long time—and we are still doing it. In spite of the consequences, in spite of the messages that come back to us, we still do it. Sometimes we do it with a straight face, as if nothing had happened. With tremendous deception, we create samsara—pain and misery for the whole world, including ourselves—but we still come off as if we were innocent. We call ourselves ladies and gentlemen, and we say, "I never commit any sins or create any problems. I'm just a regular old person, blah blah blah." That snowballing of deception and the type of existence our deception creates are shocking.

You might ask, "If everybody is involved with that particular scheme or project, then who sees the problem at all? Couldn't everybody just join in so that we don't have to see each other that way? Then we could just appreciate ourselves and our snowballing neuroses, and there would be no reference point whatsoever outside of that." Fortunately—or maybe unfortunately—we have one person who saw that there was a problem. That person was known as Buddha. He saw that there was a problem, he worked on it, and he got beyond it. He saw that the problem could be reduced—and not just reduced, but completely annihilated, because he discovered how to prevent the problem right at the source. Right at the beginning, cessation is possible.

Cessation is possible not only for the Buddha, but for us as well. We are trying to follow his path, his approach. In the twenty-six hundred years since the time of the Buddha, millions of people have followed his example, and they have been quite successful at what they were doing: they managed to become like him. The Buddha's teachings have been handed down from generation to generation, so that right now, right here, we have that information and experience. We can practice the path of meditation in the same way and style as the Buddha and our lineage ancestors. We have the transmission of the way to practice in order to overcome anxiety, deception, and neurosis. We have it and we can do it.

The Truth of Suffering

The truth of suffering should be seen

CHAPTER 1

Recognizing the Reality of Suffering

Seeing our pain as it is, is a tremendous help. Ordinarily, we are so wrapped up in it that we don't even see it. We are swimming in oceans of ice water of anxiety, and we don't even see that we are suffering. That is the most fundamental stupidity. Buddhists have realized that we are suffering, that anxiety is taking place. Because of that, we also begin to realize the possibility of salvation or deliverance from that particular pain and anxiety.

THE REALITY OF PAIN or suffering is one of the basic principles of the hinayana, the foundational teachings of Buddhism. There is suffering and pain—someone actually has to say that. It is not polite conversation; it is serious conversation: there is pain. However, unless we have an understanding and acceptance of pain, we will have no way to transcend that pain. The Sanskrit term for "suffering" is *duhkha*, which also has the sense of "anxiety." We realize that throughout our lives we are struggling. We struggle because, in our being, we feel we are what we are and cannot change. We are constantly anxious. Why? Goodness knows! Only because we have basic goodness, or innate wholesomeness, in us can we feel the counterpart of that, which is discomfort, anxiety, and confusion. In order to take a photograph, not only light but shadow is necessary.

Pain comes from anxiety, and anxiety comes from neurosis. The Sanskrit word for "neurosis" is *klesha*, and in Tibetan it is *nyönmong*.[1] *Nyön* means "stuffiness." Lots of stuffiness leads us to neurosis—*is* neurosis, in fact. In whatever we do, we experience nyönmong: when we scratch ourselves, it is nyönmong; when we eat our food, it is nyönmong; when we sit on the toilet seat, it is nyönmong; and when we smile at each other, it is nyönmong. Since we experience a sense of freakiness and unwholesomeness continuously in our ordinary life, we may begin to feel that we are being cheated. If we are theists, we get angry at God, thinking that God has cheated us; if we are nontheists, we blame karma. In either case, we feel we have been cheated by somebody, somewhere. So we begin to be resentful and doubtful, and we find that sitting on our meditation cushion is painful.

There is no relief or relaxation when we are in the samsaric world; there is always some kind of struggle going on. Even when we are supposedly enjoying life, there is still struggle and all kinds of discomfort. We may try to solve that problem by going out to restaurants or the cinema, or by enjoying our friends; nonetheless, nothing really helps. That is what is called the first noble truth, the truth of suffering. Seemingly we are trapped without hope or any way out. And once we are in that situation, we are *always* in that situation: we are in pain all the time. The Buddha's teachings do not tell us how to skip out of that pain or how to abandon it; they only say that we have to understand our state of being. The more we understand our state of being, the more we will understand why we are in pain. What we find is that the more into ourselves we are, the more we suffer, and the less into ourselves we are, the less we suffer.

Since we yearn to cure our anxiety, we are always looking for potential pleasure, but that search in itself is painful. Whenever we look for pleasure, it is always painful pleasure. Without fail, the end result is completely painful. That search for pleasure is the illogic, or bad logic, of samsaric existence. Suppose you become rich, a millionaire—along with that you collect the anxiety of losing your money, so now that you are a millionaire, you are even more anxious. Situations like that happen all the time.

Regarding pleasure from the point of view of pain is a kind of animal instinct. It is the instinct of the lower realms existing within the human situation.[2] If you do not have the reference point of pain, you cannot seem to enjoy anything. For instance, you might have bought a bottle of wine for three thousand dollars. Very painfully, you spent your three thousand dollars on this bottle of wine. So you say, "This is such fine aged wine. I paid all this money for it. Now let us have a good occasion!" But instead, it becomes a painful occasion. You worry, "What if somebody doesn't appreciate his sip of wine?" We call this "nouveau-riche samsara." Samsara is nouveau riche—it is crazy and stupid, without any dignity, and it goes on all the time.

Unless we realize the facts of life, we cannot begin to practice dharma. Being in the heat is what allows us to enjoy swimming; being in the cold is what allows us to wear nice woolen clothes. Those contradictions are natural; there is nothing extraordinary about them. Basically, we are in pain, we are suffering. Sometimes we become accustomed to our suffering, and sometimes we miss our suffering, so we deliberately invite more suffering. That is the samsaric way to exist.

The Buddhist path begins with the hinayana, which, in terms of the three-yana (or three-vehicle) journey, could be referred to as the "small vehicle" or the "immediate vehicle." The hinayana is very practical, very pragmatic. It begins with the truth of suffering: we all suffer. We rediscover that suffering or anxiety again and again. During sitting practice, that anxiety might take the form of wanting to slip into a higher level of practice, using meditation as a kind of transcendental chewing gum. During daily life, you might find that samsaric misery in your neighborhood and in your immediate surroundings; it may be connected with your relatives, your best friends, your job, or your world. Wherever you look, anxiety is always there. Your personal anxiety is what stops you from cleaning your dishes; it is what stops you from folding your shirts properly or combing your hair. Anxiety prevents you from having a decent life altogether: you are distracted by it and constantly hassled. Whether those hassles are sociological, scientific, domestic, or economic, such anxiety is very painful and always present.

Every day seems to be different; nonetheless, every day seems to be exactly the same in terms of anxiety. Basic anxiety is taking place in your everyday life all the time. When you wake up and look around, you might think of coffee or food or taking a shower; but the minute you have had your coffee or your breakfast, you realize that the anxiety is still there. In fact, anxiety is always there, hovering and haunting you throughout your life. Even though you might be extremely successful, or so-called successful, at whatever your endeavors might be, you are always anxious about something or other. You can't actually put your finger on it, but it is always there.

Seeing our pain as it is, is a tremendous help. Ordinarily, we are so wrapped up in it that we don't even see it. We are swimming in oceans of ice water of anxiety, and we don't even see that we are suffering. That is the most fundamental stupidity. Buddhists have realized that we are suffering, that anxiety is taking place. We have understood that anxiety does exist; and because of that, we also begin to realize the possibility of salvation or deliverance from that particular pain and anxiety.

According to the hinayana teachings, you have to be very practical: you are going to do something about suffering. On a very personal level, you are going to do something about it. To begin with, you could give up your scheme of what you ideally want in your life. Pleasure, enjoyment, happiness—you could give up those possibilities altogether. In turn, you could try to be kind to others, or at least stop inconveniencing others. Your existence might cause pain to somebody—you could try to stop causing that pain. As for yourself, if you find your anxiety and your desire comfortable, you could make sure that you question that perspective. In doing so, there is room for humor. As you begin to see the kind of communication that goes on between pain and pleasure, you begin to laugh. If you have too much pleasure, you can't laugh; if you have too much pain, you can't laugh; but when you are on the threshold of both pain and pleasure, you laugh. It is like striking a match.

The main point of the first noble truth is to realize that you do have such anxiousness in your being. You might be a great scholar and know the Buddhist path from top to bottom, including all the terminology—but you yourself are still suffering. You still experience basic anxiety. Look into that! At this point, we are not talking about an antidote or how to overcome that anxiety— the first thing is just to see that you are anxious. On the one hand, this is like teaching your grandmother to suck eggs, as the British say, or like teaching a bird how to fly; on the other hand, you really have to understand samsara. You are in samsara and you actually have to *realize* that.

Before you have been taught about samsara, you have no idea where you are; you are so absorbed in it that there is no reference point. Now that we are providing a reference point, look at what you are doing. Look at where you are and what you are in the midst of. That is a very important message. It is the beginning of the best enlightened message that could ever come about. At the level of *vajrayana* we might talk about the non-duality of samsara and nirvana, or fundamental wakefulness, or the flash of instantaneous liberation—but whatever we might talk about is concentrated in this very, very ordinary message: you have to review where you are. It might be a somewhat depressing prospect to realize that you are so thoroughly soaked in this greasy, heavy, dark, and unpleasant thing called samsara, but that realization is tremendously helpful. That understanding alone is the source of realizing what we call buddha in the palm of your hand—the basic wakefulness already in your possession. Such vajrayana possibilities begin at this point, right here, in realizing your samsaric anxiousness. Understanding that anxiety, which is very frustrating and not so good, is the key to realizing where you are.

The only way to work with this anxiety is the sitting practice of meditation, the taming of your mind, or *shamatha* practice. That is the basic idea of *pratimoksha*, or "individual liberation": taming yourself. The way to tame yourself, or to talk yourself out of this particular anxiety, is through the concentrated practice of shamatha discipline. The beginning of the beginning of the path of buddhadharma is about how you can actually save yourself from samsaric neurosis. You have to be very careful; you are not yet up to saving others.

In practicing buddhadharma, you cannot bypass anything. You have to begin with the hinayana and the first noble truth. Having done so, mahayana and vajrayana will come along naturally. We have to be genuine parents: instead of adopting a child who is sixty years old because we want to be the mother or father of somebody who is already accomplished, we prefer to conceive our child within our marriage. We would like to watch the birth of our child and its growth, so that finally we will have a child who is competent and good because of our training.

The progression of hinayana, mahayana, and vajrayana is well taught by the Buddha and by the lineage. If you don't have a basic foundation of hinayana, you will not understand the mahayana teachings of benevolence and loving kindness. You won't know who is being benevolent to what. You first have to experience reality, things as they are. It is like painting. First, you have to have a canvas; then, once you have the canvas properly prepared, you can paint on it—but it takes a while. The vajrayana is regarded as the final product of the best beginning; therefore, understanding the hinayana and practicing shamatha discipline are very important and powerful. You have to stick with what you have—the fact that your body, speech, and mind are in pain. The reality is that we are all trapped in samsaric neurosis, everybody, without exception. It is best that you work with reality rather than with ideals. That is a good place to begin.

CHAPTER 2

Dissecting the Experience of Suffering

The first noble truth, the truth of suffering, is the first real insight of the hinayana practitioner. It is quite delightful that such a practitioner actually has the guts, bravery, and clarity to see pain in such a precise and subtle way. We can actually divide pain into sections and dissect it. We can see it as it is, which is quite victorious. That is why it is called the truth *of* suffering.

THE PATH OF DHARMA consists of both qualities and consequences. In the Buddhist nontheistic discipline, we always work with what is there. We look into our own experience: how we feel, who we are, what we are. In doing so, we find that our basic existence is fundamentally awake and possible; but at the same time there are a lot of obstacles. The primary obstacles are ego and its habitual patterns, which manifest in all sorts of ways, most vividly and visibly in our experience of ourselves. However, before we look further into who we are or what we are, we first need to examine our fundamental notion of "self." This is also known as studying the four noble truths: the truth of suffering, the truth of the origin of suffering, the truth of the cessation of suffering, and the truth of the path.

The four noble truths are divided into two sections. The first two truths—the truth of suffering and the origin of suffering—are studies of the samsaric version of ourselves and the reasons we arrived in certain situations or came to particular conclusions about ourselves. The second two truths—the truth of cessation and the truth of the path—are studies of how we could go beyond that or overcome it. They are related with the journey and with the potentiality of nirvana, freedom, and emancipation.

Suffering is regarded as the result of samsara, and the origin of suffering as the cause of samsara. The path is regarded as the cause of nirvana, and cessation of suffering is the result. In this regard, samsara means ongoing agony, and nirvana means transcending agony and such problems as bewilderment, dissatisfaction, and anxiety.

The first noble truth is the truth of suffering. The Sanskrit word for suffering is *duhkha*. *Duhkha* could also be translated as "misery," "restlessness," "uneasiness." It is frustration. The Tibetan word for suffering is *dug-ngal*. *Dug* means "reduced into a lower level"—"wretchedness" may be the closest English word—and *ngal* means "perpetuating"; so *dug-ngal* has the sense of perpetuating that wretchedness. The quality of dug-ngal is that you have done a bad job already, and you are thriving on it and perpetuating it. It is like sticking your finger in your wound. We don't particularly *have* to suffer, but that is the way we go about our business. We start at the wrong end of the stick, and we get suffering—and it's terrible! That is not a very intelligent thing to do.

You might ask, "Who has the authority to say such a thing?" We find that the only authority who has a perspective on the whole thing is the Buddha. He discovered this; therefore, it is called the first noble truth. It is very noble and very true. He actually realized why we go about our bad job, and he pointed that out to us, which is the second noble truth. We begin to understand that and to agree with him, because we experience that there is an alternative. There is a possibility of taking another approach altogether. There is a possibility of saving ourselves from such misery and pain. It is not only possible, but it has been experienced and realized by lots of other people.

The first noble truth, the truth of suffering, is a necessary and quite delightful topic. The truth of suffering is very true and very frank, quite painfully so—and surprisingly, it is quite humorous. In order for us to understand who we are and what we are doing with ourselves, it is absolutely necessary for us to realize how we torture ourselves. The torturing process we impose on ourselves is a habitual pattern, or ape instinct. It is somewhat dependent on, or produced by, our previous lives; and at the same time, we both sustain that process and sow further karmic seeds. It is as if we were in an airplane, already flying, but while we were on board we began to plan ahead. We would like to book our next ticket so that when we reach our destination, we can immediately take off and go somewhere else. By organizing our-selves in that way, we do not actually have to stop anywhere. We are constantly booking tickets all over the place, and as a consequence we are traveling all the time. We have nowhere to stop and we don't particularly want to stop. Even if we do stop at an airport hotel, our immediate tendency is to get restless and want to fly again. So we call down to the desk and ask them to book another reservation to go somewhere else. We do that constantly, and that traveling begins to produce a lot of pain and tremendous suffering.

In terms of the notion of self, we are not actually one individual entity per se, but just a collection of what are known as the five *skandhas*, or five heaps of being (form, feeling, perception-impulse, concept, and consciousness). Within this collection, each mental event that takes place is caused by a previous one; so if we have a thought, it was produced by a previous thought. Likewise, if we are in a particular location, we were forced to be there by a previous experience; and while we are there, we produce further mental events, which perpetuate our trip into the future. We try to produce continuity. That is what is known as karma or volitional action; and from volitional action arises suffering.

The first noble truth, the truth of suffering, is the first real insight of the hinayana practitioner. It is quite delightful that such a practitioner has the guts, bravery, and clarity to see pain in such a precise and subtle way. We can actually divide pain into sections and dissect it. We can see it as it is, which is quite victorious. If we were stuck in our pain, we would have no way to talk about it. However, by telling the story of pain, we are not perpetuating pain. Instead, we have a chance to know what suffering is all about. That is quite good.

The Eight Types of Suffering

All together, we have eight kinds of suffering: birth, old age, sickness, death, coming across what is not desirable, not being able to hold on to what is desirable, not getting what we want, and general misery. Whether subtle or crude, all pain fits into those eight categories. The first four—birth, old age, sickness, and death—are based on the results of previous karma; therefore, they are called "inherited suffering." These four types of suffering are simply the hassles that are involved in being alive. The next three—coming across what is not desirable, not being able to hold on to what is desirable, and not getting what we want—are referred to as "the suffering of the period between birth and death"; and the last is simply called, "general misery."

Inherited Suffering

1. BIRTH. First there is the pain of birth. When a child is born, we celebrate its coming into our world; but at the same time, that child has gone through a lot of hassles. It is painful being born—being pushed around and pulled out. The first suffering, that of birth, may not seem valid, since nobody remembers his or her birth. It may seem purely a concept that once you were in your mother's womb feeling very comfortable swimming in warm milk and honey, sucking your thumb, or whatever you might have been doing in there. You may have conveniently forgotten your birth. But the idea is that there was a feeling of satisfaction, and then you were thrust out and had to take some kind of leap, which must have been painful.

Although you may have forgotten your birth, if you do remember or if you have watched a child experiencing the pain of birth, you see that it is very literal, ordinary, and quite frightening. As you are born, you are experiencing your first exposure to the world, which consists of hot and cold and all kinds of inconveniences. The world is beginning to try to wake you up, attempting to make you a grown-up person, but your feeling as an infant is not like that: it is a tremendous struggle. The only thing you can do is cry and rave in resentment at the discomfort.

Because you can't talk, you can't explain yourself; there is a sense of ignorance and inadequacy.

More generally, the pain of birth is based on your resistance to relating with the new demands that come at you from the world. Although it applies, first of all, to your physical birth, or the literal pain of being born, the pain of birth could also apply to your ordinary life as a grownup. That is, you are always trying to settle down in a situation in which you think that at last you've got it made. You have planned everything down to the last minute, and you don't want to change your scheme. Just like an infant settling down in its mother's womb, you don't think you ever have to come out: you do not want to deal with the hassle of being born.

This type of birth takes place all the time. In your relationships, you have decided how to deal with your friends and your lovers; economically, you feel that you have reached a comfortable level: you are able to buy a comfortable home, complete with dishwasher, refrigerator, telephone, air-conditioning, and what have you. You feel that you could stay in this womb for a long time; but then somebody comes along somewhere, and through no fault of your own—or maybe it *is* your fault—pulls the rug out from under your feet. All that careful planning you have gone through to try to remain in the womb has been interrupted. At that point, you begin to freak out right and left, talking to your friends, your lawyer, your spiritual adviser, and your financier. You wiggle around all over the place, as if you had grown ten arms and twenty legs.

You don't want to be born into the next world, but unfortunately, the situation is such that you *are* born into the next world. You might be able to save yourself a little piece, a tiny corner, but that little piece causes you so much hassle that it doesn't satisfy you all that much. Being unable to settle down in a situation is painful. You think you can settle down, but the minute you begin, you are exposed and given another birth. It is just like a baby being pushed out of its mother's womb and exposed to another world. We are not able to settle down. That is the truth.

2. OLD AGE. The second form of inherited suffering is the pain of old age. It is very inconvenient to be old. Suddenly you are incapable of doing all kinds of things, goodness knows what. Also, when you are old, you feel that you no longer have time. You no longer look forward to future situations. When you were young, you could see the whole world evolving, but now you do not have the fun and games of watching the upcoming sixty years.

Old age does not purely refer to being old; it refers to aging, to a person progressing from infanthood to old age. It is the process of things in your life slowly being changed. Over time, there is less kick taking place, less discovery or rediscovery of the world. You keep trying, but things become familiar, they have already been experienced. You may think you should try something outrageous just once, so you try that, too; but nothing really happens. It is not so much that something is wrong with your mind or with yourself, but something is wrong with your having a human body that is getting old.

An old body is physically unable to relate with things properly. As a child, you explored how to manipulate your fingers, your legs, your feet, your head, your eyes, your nose, your mouth, your ears, your hands. But at this point, everything in your system has already been explored, whatever you can use to entertain yourself on the bodily level. You haven't anything left to explore. You already know what kind of taste you are going to experience if you taste a certain thing. If you smell something, you already know exactly what it is going to smell like. You know what you are going to see, what you are going to hear, and what you are going to feel.

As we get older, we are not getting the entertainment we used to get out of things. We have already experienced practically everything that exists in our world. An old person who just came out of Tibet might experience phenomena like taking a sauna, or watching movies, or watching television as interesting, but the novelty quickly wears off. New entertainment presented to older people lasts only for a few days; whereas, for growing-up people, it might last a few years. On the day we first fell in love with somebody, it was very beautiful, but we do not get that feeling back. The day you first had ice cream was amazing, and the first day you experienced maple syrup was fantastic and great—but you have done all those things already.

Aging is very unpleasant. We realize that we have collected so much that we have become like old chimneys: all kinds of things have gone through us, and we have collected an immense thickness of soot. We are hassled and we do not want to go any further. I do not mean to insult anybody, but that is old age. And although some old people actually hold together very well, they are trying too hard.

The suffering of aging could apply to the psychological experience of aging as well as to physical aging. Initially, there is the feeling that you can do anything you want. You are appreciating your youth, dexterity, glamour, and fitness, but then you begin to find that your usual tricks no longer apply. You begin to decay, to crumble. You can't see, you can't hear, you can't walk, and you can't appreciate the things you used to enjoy. Once upon a time there was that good feeling. You could enjoy things, and certain things used to feel great. But if you try to repeat them now, in old age, your tongue is numb, your eyes are dull, your hearing is weak—your sense perceptions do not work well. The pain of old age refers to that general experience of decay.

3. SICKNESS. The third form of inherited suffering is the pain of sickness. Sickness is common to both old and young. There are all kinds of physical and semiphysical or psychological sicknesses. Sickness is largely based on the occasional panic that something might be terribly wrong with you or that you might die. It depends on how much of a hypochondriac you are. There are also occasional little polite sicknesses. You may say, "I have a cold, but I'm sure I'll get over it. I'm well, thank you, otherwise." But it is not so lighthearted as you express in your social conversation. Something more is taking place.

Sickness is an inconvenience: when you are really sick, your body becomes so much in the way that you wish you could give up the whole thing. In particular, when you check into the hospital, you feel that you have been pushed into a world full of broken glass and sharp metal points. The atmosphere of "hospitality" in hospitals is very irritating. It is not an experience of comfort and lightness. There is a sense of being helpless. One of the big themes in the Western world is to be active and helpful to yourself and not to depend on anything or anyone else, including tying your own shoelaces. So there is a lot of resentment toward that condition of helplessness.

We may experience sickness as discomfort. If we do not get good toast for breakfast, it is so irritating. The suffering of sickness includes all kinds of habitual expectations that no longer get met. Once upon a time, we used to get the things we wanted, and now they are discontinued. We would like to check with our doctor so that we can get our habitual patterns back. We want our own particular habits to keep happening, and we do not want to give anything up, viewing that as a sign of weakness. We are even threatened by not getting good toast with butter on it. We feel that the rug has been pulled out from under our feet, and a sudden panic takes place. That is a problem that the Occidental world is particularly prone to, because we are so pleasure-oriented.

Sickness, while it is largely based on pain and unfamiliarity, is also based on resentment. You resent not being entertained; and if you are thrown into unreasonable situations, such as jail, you resent the authorities. The first signs of death also tend to occur to you in sickness. When you are sick, you feel physically dejected by life, with all sorts of complaints, aches, and pains. When you get attacked by sickness, you begin to feel the loss of the beautiful wings and the nice feathers you used to have. Everything is disheveled. You can't even smile or laugh at your own jokes. You are completely demoralized and under attack.

4. DEATH. Last but not least is the pain of death. Death is the sense of not having any opportunity to continue further in your life or your endeavor—the sense of total threat. You cannot even complain: there is no authority to complain to about death. When you die, you suffer because you cannot continue with

what you want to do, or finish the unfinished work you feel you have to accomplish. There is the potential of fundamental desolation.

Death requires you to completely leave everything that you love in life, including your one and only beloved ballpoint pen. You leave all of those things. You cannot do your little habitual patterns; you cannot meet your friends anymore. You lose everything—every single item that you possess and everything you like, including the clothes you bought and your little tube of toothpaste, and the soap you like to use to wash your hands or face. All the things you personally like, all the things you appreciate for the sake of keeping yourself company, everything you enjoy in this life—every one of them completely goes. You are gone, and you cannot have them anymore. So death includes the pain of separation.

There is a further sense of pain associated with death, in that you have identified yourself so completely with your body. You can imagine losing the people you associate yourself with—your wife or husband or your closest friend—and you can imagine that when you lose your best friend or your wife or husband, you will feel completely freaked out. You can imagine such possibilities taking place in your life, but can you imagine losing your own body? When you die, you not only lose your wife or husband or friend, but you lose your body. It's terrible, absolutely ghastly. Nobody imposes that on you; you impose it on yourself. You could say, "I didn't take care of my body. I didn't eat the right food and I drank too much. I had too many cigarettes." But that does not solve the problem.

Eternally saying goodbye to our own body is very difficult. We would like to keep our body intact. If we have a cavity in our tooth or a cut in our body, we can go to our doctor and get fixed. However, when we die, that body will no longer exist. It is going to be buried or burnt and reduced to ashes. The whole thing is going to disappear, and you will have no way to identify yourself: you won't have any credit cards, and you won't have your calling cards or your driver's license. You will have no way to identify yourself if you bump into somebody who might know you.

Death is a question of leaving everything that you want, everything you so preciously possessed and hung on to—including the dharma, quite possibly. It is questionable whether you will have enough memories and imprints in your mind to return to a new situation where the Buddhist teachings are flourishing. The level of your confusion is so high that you will probably end up being a donkey. I don't want to freak you out, particularly, but that is the truth. It is the first noble truth, the straight truth, which is why we can afford to discuss these subtleties. But death is not so subtle—it is terrible to die, absolutely terrible.

You think you can fight against death. You call the doctors, priests, and philosophers and ask them for help. You look for a philosopher who has the philosophy that death doesn't exist. You look for a very competent doctor, one who has fought death millions of times, hoping you could be a candidate to be one of those who never has to go through with death. You go to a priest, who gives you communion and tells you that you will gain everlasting life. This may sound humorous, but I am afraid it is really terrifying when we come to think of it. It is terrible.

In your ordinary, everyday life you experience situations similar to death all the time. Death is an exaggeration of the previous three types of suffering. You start with birth, and having been born, you begin to settle down. You tend to put up with old age as an understandable and ongoing process, and you can relate with sickness as a natural situation. But finally you find that the whole scheme is going to end. You realize that nothing lasts very long. You are going to be dropped very abruptly, and you're going to be suddenly without breath. That is quite shocking!

Suffering of the Period between Birth and Death

Having discussed the inherited suffering of birth, old age, sickness, and death, we come to the second level of suffering. This level of suffering is related to our psychological situation and is connected with the period between birth and death. It has three categories: coming across what is not desirable; not being able to hold on to what is desirable; and not getting what we want.

We are never satisfied. We are constantly speeding around and always trying very, very hard. We never give up. We always try to get the few leftover peanuts out of the corner of the can.

5. COMING ACROSS WHAT IS NOT DESIRABLE. The first category is the pain of coming across what is not desirable. Our attitude to life is usually quite naive: we think that we can avoid meeting ugly or undesirable situations. Usually we are quite tricky and quite successful at avoiding such things. Some people have tremendous problems and experience one disaster after another, but they still try to avoid them. Other people have led their lives quite successfully, but even they sometimes find that their tricks don't work. They are suddenly confronted with a situation that is completely the opposite of what they want. They say, "Terrible! Good heavens! I didn't expect that! What happened?" Then, quite conveniently, they blame somebody else, if they have a scheming enough style of thinking; and if they don't, they just freak out with their mouths open.

6. NOT BEING ABLE TO HOLD ON TO WHAT IS DESIRABLE. The second category is the opposite of that. It is the pain of trying to hold on to what is desirable, fantastic, lovely, splendid, terrific. It is as if you are trying to hold on to a good situation, and suddenly there is a leak. What you are holding in your arms and cherishing so much begins to fizzle out like a balloon. When that occurs, you begin to be very resentful or try to see it as somebody else's problem.

7. NOT GETTING WHAT YOU WANT. Underlying the previous two categories is the third, which is that, on the whole, we can't get what we want. That is the case. You might say, "One day I'm going to become a great movie star, a millionaire, a great scholar, or at least a decent person. I would like to lead my life happily ever after. I have this plan. I'm going to be either a saint or a sinner, but I'm going to be happy." However, none of those situations happen. And even if you do become a great movie star or a millionaire, something else crops up, so that being such a

person doesn't help. You begin to realize that there are further problems with your life and that, on the whole, your life is very grim. Nothing will satisfy you. Nothing will be wish-fulfilling at all, absolutely not. Something is not quite working. Whether you are smart or dumb, it doesn't make much difference: things don't quite work. That creates tremendous anxiety, chaos, and dissatisfaction.

General Misery

8. ALL-PERVASIVE SUFFERING. The last category, all-pervasive suffering—is quite a different form of suffering altogether. The previous seven were understandable situations of pain and suffering. Number eight is not worse, but more subtle. It is the subtle sense of general misery and dissatisfaction that goes on all the time—completely all the time. This general misery that exists in us is not recognized; there is just a sense that we are in our own way. We feel that we are an obstacle to ourselves and to our own success. There is a sense of heaviness, hollowness, and wretchedness, which is eternal. If you are having the greatest time in your life, a moment of fantastic enjoyment, there's still an edge to it. Things are not one hundred percent fulfilled. You can't fully relax without referring to the past or the future. A big sigh has been taking place all the time, ever since you were born.

General misery, or all-pervasive suffering, is based on the inheritance of neurosis. Even when we experience joy or pleasure in our lifetime, if we do at all, that pleasure has a tinge of sourness in it. In other words, sourness is part of the definition of pleasure. We cannot experience just one thing, without having some contrast to it. That is the highest experience of spirituality: there is a little bit of sweet and sour always.

All-pervasive suffering is connected with constant movement: flickering thoughts, latching onto one situation after another, or constantly changing subjects. It is like getting out of a car and walking into a building, and getting out of the building and walking into a car, and being hungry and settling down in a restaurant and eating food, and going back. It is connected with what you are doing right now.

Our life consists of a lot of shifts. After boredom, such shifts may seem pleasurable and entertaining. For instance, if we have had a long ride, getting out of the car is good; getting out of the car and walking into a restaurant is better; ordering food is better still; and ordering some liquor or dessert is best of all, great. At such times, things seem good, and you are experiencing nothing wrong in your life. Everything is ideal, fine. There is nothing to complain about and everything is solid and fantastic. But even in that kind of feeling, an element of pain still exists. That sense of satisfaction is largely based on no longer feeling the pain that you experienced before.

It is questionable how much we are dealing with previous experiences and how much we are ready to deal with life in terms of oncoming new experiences. Quite possibly, we will find that we fit even new experiences into our old categories. In doing so, we do not experience satisfaction, but pain. In Buddhism, satisfaction is minute. When we are satisfied, we may have a sense of accomplishment and self-snugness; but at the same time, there is also a sense of that being questionable. So we are never fully satisfied.

This last form of suffering, general misery, is supposedly so subtle that it can only be perceived by realized ones. Only they have a sense of contrast to that anxiety, a sense of the absence of anxiety. However, although it has been said that this form of suffering is very difficult for people to understand, it is not really all that sophisticated. It is actually very simple. The point is that ordinarily you are immune to your own suffering. You have been suffering for such a long time that you don't notice it unless you are attacked by very vivid or very big problems. In that way, you are like somebody who is very heavy. A three-hundred-pound person may be quite jolly and happy because he feels that all that weight is part of his body. He doesn't feel that carrying this big heavy weight is particularly painful until he begins to have shortened breath or thoughts of heart problems.

Likewise, you are immune to your own suffering. Since you carry your burden of suffering with you all the time, you have grown accustomed to it. You have learned to live with it. On the whole, even though you carry this burden of fixation, which constantly perpetuates your mental events of disaster, you do not recognize it. You are immune to the disaster of the kleshas— the negative, unwholesome mental confusions of aggression, passion, and ignorance that make you stupid and keep you wandering around. You are immune to the general sense of suffering that takes place all the time.

Three Patterns of Suffering

The eight types of suffering were previously divided into inherited suffering, the suffering of the period between birth and death, and general misery. However, suffering can also be described in terms of three patterns: the suffering of suffering, the suffering of change, and all-pervasive suffering.

The suffering of suffering includes the categories of birth, old age, sickness, death, and coming across what is not desirable. It is known as the suffering of suffering because first you have birth, which is terribly painful, and on top of that you have sickness, old age, and death. Having been born, you get all of that lumped on you; and on top of that, you come across things that are not desirable. Since all of those sufferings are piled up in that way, this is called the suffering of suffering. An analogy is that you have cancer, and on top of that you go bankrupt, and your house collapses on you.

The suffering of change includes two categories: trying to hold on to what is desirable; and not getting—or not knowing— what you want.[1] In the first case, you discover something desirable and then it is gone. In the second, you are unable to discover what you want, which causes you tremendous anxiety. Either you fail to find out what you really want or it keeps changing. An analogy for the suffering of change is being at your wedding reception and having a bomb explode in the middle of the dining room table. A milder analogy is having a great dinner and finding that the dessert is a disaster. The suffering of changeability includes anything that has a good beginning and a sour ending.

All-pervasive suffering is the eighth type of suffering, or general misery. Our condition is basically wretched because of the burden of the five skandhas, which perpetuate our neuroses and our habitual thought patterns. Because of that, we begin to find that, on the whole, we have never experienced any real happiness.

There is one particular point that I would like to make: there is no such thing as real happiness. It's a myth. In the way we go about it, there is no such thing as real happiness at all. We've been striving so hard for it, trying all the time to cultivate so much goodness, so many pleasures—but we started at the wrong end of the stick from the very beginning. Something went wrong as we began ourselves. We are trying to entertain ourselves in the wrong way—by having an ego, by having fixation. But we can't get any pleasure out of fixation; and after that, the whole thing goes down the drain. However, we could start at the right end of the stick, without fixation, without clinging—that is always possible. That is what is called the second half of the four noble truths: the truth of cessation and the truth of the path.

By the way, the first noble truth is not quite the same as the theistic concept of original sin. You have not failed, and you are not being punished or thrown in jail. You just started at the wrong end of the stick. Therefore, what you experience is a general sense of pain, whose source you cannot find. If you could find out where it came from, you could probably solve it, but you haven't been able to do so. In contrast, the right end of the stick means starting properly, with lots of discipline. By becoming more sensitive to all-pervasive suffering, you have a chance to overcome it.

All together, lots of hassles take place. Having been born is very painful, and having a body is also extraordinarily painful. On top of that, we are sick until we die. We die because we are sick. Since we were born, we have never been cured; otherwise, we could not die. In whatever we do, even at the highest level of pleasure, there is always a tinge of pain. So pain is almost the entire consistency of our life, the water we make our soup out of, our life in detail.

In regard to suffering, to pain and pleasure, whenever an element of sanity begins to take place, the neurotic pain is lessened and becomes somewhat less dramatic and personal. At the same time, because of the clarity of mind, the pain itself becomes more pronounced—not because the pain is more, but because the confusion is less. Therefore, with greater clarity, pain is experienced more harshly, more precisely and directly. According to the *abhidharma*, the Buddhist teachings on psychology and philosophy, the unwise feel pain as the stroke of a hair on the hand, but the wise feel pain as the stroke of a hair on the eye. So the wise feel much more pain, because they are freer from neurosis. They feel *real* pain and the real precision of pain. Jamgön Kongtrül says that the ultimate understanding of pain is that you cannot get rid of your pain, but you can have a higher understanding of pain. That seems to be how things go.

At this point, we are dealing with the brass-tacks level. At the beginning, at the hinayana level, Buddhism is somewhat crude, but it is presentable to people. There is the notion of pain and misery, and the notion that we can actually save ourselves from that misery if we practice the teachings. That may be crude, but it is true, and it makes sense to people. It is very real and honest. You can't psychologize the whole thing by saying, "You have pain, but regard it as nonexistence," and then just go about your philosophical discussion. That approach doesn't help very much, so you have to stick to the level of primitive truth. And if you look into it subtly, you realize that it is not all that primitive, but it is very, very sophisticated. You have to present dharma as a workable situation; otherwise, it is not actually communicable to anybody, and it becomes a fairy tale. You could say, "Sit and practice. Then you will be out of your misery." It is not exactly a promise, or something you have up your sleeve, but it is true. Very simple.

In discussing the first noble truth, we are not saying that somebody should not be born, should never get sick, should never get old, and should never die. However, in regard to the *suffering* of those things, a person can experience death without pain, sickness without pain, old age without pain, and birth without pain. We are not concerned with going against the laws and norms of the phenomenal world. We would never have any Buddhists if they were not born. So I'm afraid that you are stuck with birth, death, old age, and sickness. You can overcome the pain aspect of it, but you cannot overcome the totality.

The hinayanists said that about the Buddha himself: that he was born and he died, so he was still subject to the samsaric norm, to some extent. He was purely *nirmanakaya*, or on the earth; he was not a superman. He was a good person, but he still had to stick with the worldly norms: he had to eat his food and he had to die. And we have the same situation. We're not trying to go beyond that. We're not trying to refute any scientific laws.

We can actually declare that, as nontheistic Buddhists, we can free the whole world from pain. That's the greatest news. And we are doing it properly, rather than by worshiping somebody or going into a trance. We are doing it methodically, scientifically, psychologically. Starting with ourselves, we are expanding that news to others in turn. It is very definite and ordinary—and at the same time, it is quite remarkable.

The Truth of the Origin of Suffering

The origin of suffering should be avoided

CHAPTER 3

The Power of Flickering Thoughts

Everything starts on a minute scale at the beginning and then expands. Things begin to swell and expand until they become very large—immeasurably large, in a lot of cases. We can experience that ourselves. Minute shifts of attention are what create the emotions of aggression, passion, ignorance, and all the rest. Although those emotions are seemingly very heavy-handed, large-scale, and crude, they have their origin in the subtle twists that take place in our mind constantly.

SUFFERING, THE FIRST of the four noble truths, comes from absentmindedness; it comes from stupidity or ignorance. We are not fundamentally incapable of being mindful, but we are unable to develop exertion or striving on the path. Absentmindedness, not being aware, brings a sense of "lost and split," and that sense of basic confusion naturally brings pain. Because of that sense of dissatisfaction, of not finding your right place, you try to attack the world outside or to complain—but actually, the complaint should be on yourself. The original problem began because you lost your awareness. You cannot lay that on someone else.

The basic quality of suffering is that you cannot behave in the proper manner. The first glimpse of suffering is a sense of clumsiness: you are unable to coordinate your body, speech, and mind. That sense of complete clumsiness can be referred to as "ape instinct." From suffering comes the notion of irritation. Because you are not quite in accordance with your environment, the world begins to attack you. You may sit in a very uncomfortable chair, which simply doesn't fit you, so you feel painfully cramped. You may step in some dog shit on the pavement, and suddenly you have no idea whom to blame: the dog who shat, yourself, or the uncleanness of the city. There is an ongoing bewilderment or grudge against the world. You are supposed to say something to somebody who attacks you—but you have created the inconvenience yourself, so you do not know what to do. Basically, any movement you make by not being aware creates suffering and pain. Losing track, losing context, losing a reference point of openness brings pain.

Understanding suffering is very important. The practice of meditation is designed not to develop pleasure but to understand the truth of suffering; and in order to understand the truth of suffering, one also has to understand the truth of awareness. When true awareness takes place, suffering does not exist. Through awareness, suffering is somewhat changed in its perspective. It is not necessarily that you do not suffer, but the haunting quality that fundamentally you are in trouble is removed. It is like removing a splinter. It might hurt, and you might still feel pain, but the basic cause of that pain, the ego, has been removed.

The second noble truth is about the origin of suffering: how suffering and dissatisfaction arise. Suffering begins with very simple and ordinary flickers of thought, which derive from basic bewilderment. Before intention begins, there is a state of utter uncertainty, in the sense of a generally dull and stupefied state of mind. That uncertainty or bewilderment occurs every fraction of a second in our state of being. It goes on all the time. We don't know whether we are coming or going, perceiving or not perceiving. Due to that uncertainty, we prefer to spin in circles rather than to look around and extend outward. Our actions are colored or flavored by a kind of fundamental ape instinct; our only guidance is our own very fermented body odor or mind odor. It is like the blind leading the blind. We are just sniffing around. In this stupefied state, you are willing to step into a corral or den, like an animal, not knowing that the consequences will be painful. In that way, you are drawn toward pain rather than toward pleasure.

That tendency toward pain comes not from either pain or pleasure but from wanting to bury your head in yourself and smell your own wickedness. You would rather stick with your family than go out and meet strangers. You prefer to relate with your own nest, which happens to be a bad choice, and the result is pain. So you start with ignorance, which is very self-snug, like living in a cocoon. Due to ignorance, you prefer to let a gigantic growth develop in you rather than be operated on and feel better, because the operation is too painful, and it is too big a deal to do anything about it. You even take pride in that approach. However, although you are looking for pleasure, it turns out to be pain. For you, basic goodness has not yet come up. Basic goodness is like getting up and taking a shower, which wakes you up; but you would rather not do that, even though you have a bathroom. You prefer to doze in your bed. It's less of a hassle and you don't have to sacrifice or give anything up. It is much easier just to swim around in your dirt. You don't take a shower, you don't wash, you don't go to the barber and cut your hair, you just grow a long beard and long hair and kick around with your own little pleasure. This is as close as we can get to the notion of samsara.

Within that stupidity you begin to find something, and that something is passion or lust. You don't even know what you are lusting for, but you are willing to indulge yourself. Desire or lust is that which ignites. It is based on wanting to build yourself up. But you do not need desire. You could take a walk with the desire of building yourself up, but you could also take a walk without trying to build yourself up. You could just take a walk, very simply and straightforwardly. Doing so would be very opening. There doesn't have to be a second meaning all the time, and you don't have to philosophize everything. There could be pure motivation.

The natural, instinctive yearning toward pain is known as *künjung* in Tibetan, and in Sanskrit it is *samudaya*. *Kün* means "all" or "every," and *jung* means "arising," so *künjung* means "the origin of all." Künjung is an abbreviation for *nyönmong künjung*, which means "the origin of all the defilements (kleshas)." It is where all the defilements and pain are created. Künjung gives birth to the twelve *nidanas*, the links in the chain of causation (ignorance, formation, consciousness, name and form, the six senses, contact, feeling, craving, clinging, becoming, birth, and death). It is the origin of the five skandhas, which are permeated with kleshas.

According to the abhidharma, künjung can arise as flickering thoughts and is connected with the notion of *semjung*, the fifty-one mental events arising from the mind. Künjung is also associated with two forms of *drippa*, or obscuration: *pakchak kyi drippa*, the "obscuration of habitual tendencies," and *nyönmong kyi drippa*, the "obscuration of negative emotions." The flickering is pakchak kyi drippa, which sets off the emotions, or nyönmong kyi drippa. The flickering acts like the pilot light on your stove, which is always on and sets off all the rest of the burners. Likewise, there is always some pakchak kyi drippa waiting to light any of the skandhas or kleshas, which are ready and waiting to be lit up.

The idea of künjung, the origin of suffering, is that it progresses. When we project ourselves into a situation or into a particular world, we begin with a very small and minute shift of attention; and from that, things become enlarged and exaggerated. According to the abhidharma, the connection between small ideas and large ideas is very important. For instance, sudden dramas, such as murdering somebody or creating immense chaos, begin on the level of minute concepts and tiny shifts of attention. Something large is being triggered by something quite small. The first little hint of dislike or attraction for somebody eventually escalates and brings on a much more immense scale of emotional drama or psychodrama. So everything starts on a minute scale, at the beginning, and then expands. Things begin to swell and expand until they become very large—immeasurably large, in a lot of cases. We can experience that ourselves. Such minute shifts of attention are what create the emotions of aggression, passion, ignorance, and all the rest. Although those emotions are seemingly very heavy-handed, large-scale, and crude, they have their origin in the subtle twists that take place in our mind constantly.

Because of that sudden shiftiness of attention, and because our minds are basically so untrained, we begin to have a sense of casualness about the whole thing. We are constantly looking for possibilities of either possessing someone, destroying someone, or conning somebody into our world. That struggle is taking place all the time. The problem is that we have not properly related with the shiftiness. We experience the arising of such thoughts right now, all the time; otherwise the second noble truth wouldn't be truth—it would just be theory.

It is possible for people who have been practicing meditation and studying the teachings, who are opened up and intrigued, to see this pattern. If you have been practicing, you are somewhat raw and unskinned, which is good; although if you are too ripe, you might want to run away or try to grow thicker skin. Being able to relate with the subtleties of mental shifts is connected with the hinayana principle of paying attention to every activity that we do in smaller doses. There is no such thing as sudden psychodrama without any cause and effect. Every psychodrama that takes place in our mind or in our actions has its origin in little flickering thoughts and little flickerings of attention.

CHAPTER 4

The Development of Set Patterns

One way to deal with suffering is to understand its mechanics, how it develops and functions. If we immediately discuss the cure, that doesn't particularly help. First, you have to slow down and take the time to understand or realize the second noble truth, the origin of suffering. There is no other cure for suffering at this point, except to understand its makeup and psychology.

THE ORIGIN OF SUFFERING, strangely, can come either from trying to be highly disciplined and aware or from completely losing one's awareness. Generally, if you are not mindful and aware, suffering begins to arise; whereas, if you are mindful and aware, suffering does not arise. However, suffering can also come from using your awareness discipline as a means of securing yourself by developing set patterns in life.

Ego-oriented patterns arise from both attitudes and actions, and lead to suffering. They include (1) regarding the five skandhas as belonging to oneself, (2) protecting oneself from impermanence, (3) believing that one's view is best, (4) believing in the extremes of nihilism and eternalism, (5) passion, (6) aggression, and (7) ignorance.

Regarding the Five Skandhas as Belonging to Oneself

The first set pattern is regarding the five skandhas (form, feeling, perception-impulse, concept, and consciousness) as belonging to oneself. This is known as "the bad view," or "the view that is not so good."

Protecting Oneself from Impermanence

The second set pattern, held by a lot of people, is protecting oneself from impermanence and trying to develop eternal life. Believing that you are or could be eternal, the first thing you do is to seek the wrong kind of master, someone who promises, "If you practice my way, I will give you eternal life. You will live forever!" It's the old Shangri-la approach. Although you know that your body cannot last forever, you hope at least to make your spirit last forever by seeking a spiritual master and asking to be saved.

Believing That One's View Is the Best

The third set pattern is believing that one's view is the best. It is based on a spiritually materialistic approach to holiness. You think, "This place is sacred, this body is sacred, and this practice is sacred," but that feeling of holiness is founded on the very confused ground of spiritual materialism. It is based on the belief that some magical power is going to save you.

Believing in the Extreme of Nihilism or Eternalism

The fourth set pattern is believing in the extreme of nihilism or eternalism. In the extreme of nihilism, everything is regarded as completely empty, nothing. Nothing in your life matters. Whatever happens—whether you are on the beach or in the mountains, watching the sunset or the sunrise, seeing birds fly or flowers grow, hearing bees hum—nothing really matters.

The extreme of nihilism comes from the philosophical belief that if you don't believe in anything at all, you are free from everything. It is connected with the *shunyata* experience of no form, no speech, no emotions, and so forth. Every experience is completely philosophized. That nihilistic philosophy is reinforced by saying that you should appreciate everything as an expression of emptiness. For example, you listen to the sound of the ash falling from the incense stick as the sound of emptiness, as shunyata. By appreciating things as an expression of emptiness, you think everything is going to be okay.

In the extreme of eternalism, you think that everything is everlasting and secure. However, instead of just thinking everything is going to be okay, you feel that you have to make a connection with what is happening around you. You feel that you have to be one with the earth and the trees, one with nature, which is eternal. Purely enjoying something, appreciating it, and saying nothing is a problem, doesn't help—you have to get into the details and make it more personal. You have to eat the right food, do the right kind of exercises, wear the right kind of clothes. You have to get into the right kind of yin and yang rhythm. You believe in an eternal norm or law that governs our lives, and the idea is that you should connect with that, be on the right side of the cosmos, so that you do not have any problems or hassles.

Once you begin to believe in one of those two extremes, you feel that you do not need to sit and meditate; instead, meditation comes to you. Unfortunately, that is not quite true. Something *else* comes to you: the belief in nihilism or eternalism. Although that may be a pleasant experience, temporarily speaking, without a definite practice and discipline taught by a lineage holder in an authentic tradition, you cannot solve the nihilist or the eternalist extreme or transcend the origin of suffering. Practice brings a sense of presence and simple awareness, so that experience is very real, rather than having either a nihilistic or eternalistic shadow behind it to make everything feel solid. In terms of nihilism, instead of saying, "Yes, the sun rose. Sure. So what?" you simply say, "The sun rose!" And in terms of eternalism, rather than saying, "I had a macrobiotic meal for my dinner," you simply say, "So what? I had food!" The hinayana level of consciousness is very profound.

This is a very simplified version of nihilism and eternalism. The philosophers and theologians of Hinduism talk about these two extremes in a very sophisticated way; however, at this point, we are presenting these two views in terms of contemporary eternalists and nihilists who live in California or New York City. Basically, both eternalism and nihilism are ways of trying to nourish one's existence and one's ego. They are extreme views in the sense that either you couldn't care less and nothing is a problem, or there *is* a problem, so you have to be on the right side of it. In relating to these two extremes, the point is neither to abandon both extremes nor to believe in both. Instead, you have to develop an entirely different system of thinking in which there is no security and no ego. Only awareness brings a real sense of that nondual approach.

Passion, Aggression, and Ignorance

The last set pattern is a very familiar group: passion, aggression, and ignorance. Passion or lust, strangely enough, has a very interesting psychological back-and-forth play with aggression. That is, the problem of passion comes from its not being pure and complete passion, which would be straightforward and true. The passion or lust we experience in the realm of ego is quite the opposite. There is a touch of hatred in it, which brings wantingness, grasping, and possessiveness. You feel that you don't have something, so you want to grasp it. You think, "Because I feel that I am not really here, I feel this pain. How can I maintain myself properly?" And the instruction you get from yourself is that in order to be passionate, you have to be slightly aggressive. Similarly, in aggression, there is a faint sense of desire and lust, which makes the aggression more powerful. So having an aggressive attitude to somebody is equal to having a love affair with somebody. As far as ignorance is concerned, it has elements of both passion and aggression: the desire to learn is mixed with a faint touch of hatred. You think your state of mind may not be intelligent enough to know; therefore, you begin to ignore what you might know and develop hatred toward knowledge and learning.

These seven set views, or set patterns, are the basic constituents of the origin of suffering. Once we have fallen into any one of them, or all of them, we experience constant struggle, competition, pain, and confusion. If we approach the second noble truth with the flavor of contemplative practice, we find that these basic constituents are obvious and personal.

As a practitioner, you realize that these patterns don't particularly go away, but at least you know what they are all about, and as you go along, you will probably know what you should do about it. You may think that once the dharma or the truth has been spoken, it should solve those problems automatically, but that is not the case. First you have to get into the dharma; *then* you can think about what you can do. Unless you are a businessman, you can't discuss bankruptcy.

CHAPTER 5

Perpetually Re-creating Suffering

Our habitual pattern is that whenever we encounter any-thing undesirable and unappealing, we try little ways within ourselves to avoid it. We could watch ourselves doing that. The little things we do, the little areas in which we try to entertain ourselves—that process which takes place all the time is both the product of suffering and the producer of suffering. It is the origin that perpetually re-creates suffering, as well as what we are constantly going through as the result of suffering.

THE ORIGIN OF SUFFERING, künjung, is based on the belief in eternity. That belief in eternity marks the difference between theism and nontheism. Out of the belief in eternity comes the hope of maintaining oneself, of continuing to be, and the search for longevity of the self, or ego. Along with that comes a fear of death. We look for all sorts of alternatives, for some way to occupy ourselves. We keep groping around in order to survive. That groping process is connected with the development of the kleshas. We begin to look outward from ourselves to others, out into the world, and grasp at the world as a way of maintaining ourselves. We use the world as a crutch. That process leads to suffering, as a result, because the various ways we try to maintain ourselves do not actually help to maintain us—in fact, they hinder us—so our scheme begins to break down. The more it breaks down, the more we have to rebuild; and as that rebuilding takes place, the suffering returns, so again and again we go back to rebuilding. It is a vicious cycle. The process of samsara goes on and on. We have to understand its workings, for once we know how samsara operates, we will know how to work with it. We will know what to overcome and what to cultivate.

The path or journey becomes important because it breaks down fixation—holding on to oneself and holding on to others—which could be said to be the origin of suffering. There are two types of künjung: the künjung of kleshas and the künjung of karma. The kleshas are one's state of being, one's state of mind. Kleshas such as passion, aggression, arrogance, and ignorance are all internal situations; they are purely mental events. The künjung of karma is acting upon others as a result of such kleshas. Both types of künjung could be considered karmic; however, the second type of künjung is much more karmic because it involves making decisions, dealing with others, and actually doing something with the phenomenal world.

The künjung of kleshas could be said to be an embryonic expression of the künjung of karma. As an example, if something pops into your mind as you are meditating and you recognize it immediately, it does not have the same karmic weight as if you had acted upon it. Once you see through it, it is just a game rather than a serious plan that you have; whereas, if you write it down in your little notebook so you can remember to call your friend and tell her about it, you have already planted a karmic seed. Simply perceiving it through your mind and seeing the futility of it, realizing it is just a game, is the saving grace. That seems to be the point of the practice of meditation.

The Six Root Kleshas: Conflicting Emotions That Lead to Suffering

Kleshas are defilements or conflicting emotions. There are six root kleshas and twenty secondary kleshas.[1] Kleshas are minute at the beginning, but their consequences are large and disastrous. The origin of conflicting emotions is that you are jumpy and always looking for entertainment. Kleshas seem magically to manifest out of the blue and come to your attention, but they do so because you are ready for them. Having already created an object to direct your attention to, you develop further confusion, in which desirable things are seen as undesirable, and undesirable things are seen as desirable. That little perversion takes place; the process is slightly twisted. You do not know who you are or what your actual desires are. There are of all kinds of possibilities, but with all of them, there is a slight twist, which could be described as mistaken perception. Out of this basic mental setup, passion, aggression, ignorance, and all kinds of subsidiary emotions begin to arise.

Traditional texts describe the nature of emotions as disturbance and chaos. Conflicting emotions are the ups and downs and irregularities that take place in your mind. There are supposedly six root emotions: desire, anger, pride, ignorance, doubt, and opinion.[2] Those six kleshas are known as "that which disturbs tranquillity," as if there were any tranquillity at all when you are bogged down in the samsaric world. Generally, we have a very hard time finding any little space in which to have the experience of tranquillity or peace. Tranquillity is simply a temporary relief from indulging in one of those six states of being.

The six root kleshas arise in succession out of basic stupidity or bewilderment. That is, from the bewilderment of not knowing what to do comes a sudden flickering of thoughts. That begins to make you very passionate and lustful. So the first klesha is *desire*. Actually, it is more like lust than desire. You become horny about yourself and your state of bewilderment. Then, since you are unable to experience the proper fulfillment of that horniness, you experience *anger*. Out of that anger and inability to fulfill yourself comes arrogance or *pride*, as a kind of self-preservation or self-maintenance. After that comes carelessness, uncertainty, or *ignorance*. This ignorance is a different sort of ignorance than the initial triggering process. It is not basic bewilderment but rather simply boycotting situations, ignoring things, refusing to see things in an intelligent way. So passion leads to aggression, which leads to pride, which leads to a stupidified sort of noncaring. Those are the first four kleshas.

Ignoring then develops into the fifth klesha, which is known as *doubt*. You do not trust any possible alternatives and do not want advice or any way out. You doubt the teachings, the teacher, and the buddhadharma. You even doubt the simple, sensible norms of everyday existence. From that comes the sixth klesha, which is known as view, or *opinion*. You form a certain opinion, which you use to solidify your trip. You say, "This is it. I've got it. I know it, and I refuse to believe anything else. This is my view; this is my idea; this is what I have come to believe is the right thing to do."

In terms of the künjung of kleshas, it has been said that ignorance is the source of suffering; it has also been said that passion is the origin of suffering, but there is no particular conflict between those two views. Passion refers to the confusion of always wanting to grasp the next possible situation. By continuously clinging to situations, we perpetually give birth to desire. So passion is a driving, impulsive force; but underlying that is a sense of uncertainty, bewilderment, and ignorance. So the origin of suffering could also be said to be fundamental ignorance. The term *fundamental* refers to the ground in which we find ourselves suffering. Basic bewilderment and suffering are existence. They *are*. They don't have any partnership, they just *are*. You are your own suffering, your own ignorance. The klesha of ignorance (*timuk*) is just superficial bewilderment. In contrast, fundamental ignorance (*avidya*) is the refusal to relate at all with the totality of suffering. You want to boycott the whole situation.

Karmic Patterns That Lead to Suffering

The origin of suffering as karma is quite simple and definite. It begins with ignorance; ignorance is, therefore, the origin. Ignorance, in turn, causes volitional action. From volitional action, the entire chain reaction of karma, one nidana after another, can take place. So we have the concept of a karmic chain reaction— not only the concept, but the fact of karma begins to be born in our world and in our life.

Both psychological states or attitudes and the physical environment bring about karmic consequences. The karmic force that exists in our ordinary everyday life is unavoidable. If we are poor, it is unlikely that suddenly we will become rich—although if we are rich, we may find it easy to suddenly become poor! If we are young, we cannot suddenly be old; if we are old, we cannot suddenly become young. Those self-existing situations that we are stuck with are expressions of the origin of suffering. We are stuck with them and we have no choice. Not only have we no choice, but we have to deal with them, which is a hassle. That is a karmic problem. Beyond that, depending on how we handle ourselves, we can continue to create further debts, or we can try not to create further debts. How we handle that depends on our state of existence and on our ordinary, everyday life. We are stuck in our particular world because of such karmic patterns, and we find ourselves involved in trying to perpetuate pleasure and cool down pain, even down to the most remote little details. If we feel discomfort, we might pick up a Life Saver and put it in our mouth and try to live on that for a few seconds, or we might take a cigarette and light it, or we might decide to stand up and stretch our legs and turn around and look out the window. All those little gestures are expressions that we are subject to some kind of problem. But we are only perpetuating that problem by indulging in more unnecessary activity. However, that does not mean that one should not take Life Savers or stand up and look out the window—that would be too simple. But our habitual pattern is that whenever we encounter anything undesirable and unappealing, we try little ways within ourselves to avoid it.

We could watch ourselves doing that. The little things we do, the little areas in which we try to entertain ourselves—that process which takes place all the time—is both the product of suffering and the producer of suffering. It is the origin that perpetually re-creates suffering, as well as what we are constantly going through as the result of suffering. From that point of view, everything is extraordinarily hopeless. However, it is better to take that attitude of hopelessness than to view the whole thing as a big joke. Regarding everything as a big joke is an adharmic, or anti-Buddhist, approach. It is freestyle Buddhism. So we should stick to facts and figures, to what we are going through in our life. We are all subject to these problems, and we ought to realize that and try to understand it. Later on, we may be able to relate to the third noble truth, the truth of cessation, and look into how we can be inspired. But for now it is better to be very realistic. That is absolutely important.

Unmeritorious Karma

The künjung of karma can be divided into unmeritorious karma and meritorious karma. Unmeritorious karma comes from a seed of fundamental aggression. It is not based on a polite form of aggression but comes from a deeper level of resentment and anger. Even before you start to act or begin to create suffering, you have all sorts of wicked desires to plant bad karmic seeds.

UNMERITORIOUS KARMA CONNECTED WITH THE BODY. The unmeritorious karma arising from fundamental aggression is composed of what are known as the ten evil acts, which are divided into three sections: body, speech, and mind. The first three acts, which are related to body, are *taking life, stealing,* and *sexual misconduct.* They are a mixture of passion and aggression. The first two, taking life and stealing, are connected with aggression. The third one, sexual misconduct, is connected with passion—or possibly with aggression, depending upon one's outlook on the world. All three are attempts to bring the outer world into your own wicked world. You are trying to build some kind of empire, based on your own version of things. Taking life, stealing, and sexual misconduct are conditioned by ulterior motives of all kinds. If you can't work with somebody, you reject him: you try to kill him or you try to steal from him. And if you accept somebody, if you include him in your territory, you try to have sex with him. It's a very immediate way of dealing with situations.

Sometimes we put animals in cages and study them—how they eat, how they mate, how they produce babies, how they bring up their young. But in fact, we don't need to put animals in a cage; we can watch ourselves do all those things. We are already in a samsaric cage, and we are a perfect zoological study. Life in samsara is very crude. If we had some other perspective, it might be seen as quite embarrassing; but since we have no other perspective, the whole thing is accepted. Taking life, stealing, and sexual misconduct are regulated by social norms. Some forms of these actions are approved by law because they go along with the basic scheme of society; others are not approved by law because they interfere with that scheme. But all of them, whether lawful or unlawful, are connected with the scheme of rejecting and accepting. It all boils down to that.

UNMERITORIOUS KARMA CONNECTED WITH SPEECH. The next four of the ten evil acts are connected with speech. Number four is *telling lies*. You want to defend your particular cause, so you try to deceive. Telling lies is connected with a mixture of passion and aggression: you are trying to reject somebody and to include them in your world, both at the same time. Lying, in this context, means telling elaborate, obvious lies, with the intention to promote your own prosperity or your own security.

Number five is *intrigue*, which is based on trying to divide. When you find that the world is too solid, that it has developed a united front against you, you try to break it down by intrigue. You make somebody your friend and somebody else your enemy. You try to win by drawing some people to yourself and putting off others.

Number six is *negative words*. You feel that you can proclaim tremendous wisdom by speaking critically of somebody or some particular topic. You speak harsh words. You hope that if you speak your harsh words loudly and clearly, they will be a kind of weapon or bomb that you can throw into the midst of society, into the midst of your friends, or into the midst of your enemies. You hope that your words will give you power over others. As the creator of harsh, destructive words, you hope that you can destroy society, concepts, ideas, feelings, and theories of all kinds.

Number seven is *gossip*, or, for that matter, anything other than functional talk. You gossip in order to pervert others, in order to destroy those who have developed great exertion and discipline. You would like to break their discipline and bring them down to your level by talking about crocodiles and the weather and your idea of their idea. Such chatter has a tremendously evil effect on others because it is so effective. It does not provide sharp points; it just lures others into further discursive thought. It lures others into chattering. We know that there are a lot of people who are experts at that.

UNMERITORIOUS KARMA CONNECTED WITH THE MIND. The last three of the ten evil acts are connected with mind. Number eight is *envy*, which is connected with wishful thinking and poverty mentality. You have so much desire to grasp what you don't have, yet you feel inadequate to do so. You envy other people's situations. You feel basically inferior, that you have less wisdom, less clarity of mind, less skillful means, less concentration, less whatever it might be. When you look at somebody who has slightly more than you, you feel greedy, completely hurt. You feel bad if somebody else has a good idea or if somebody has tremendous vision, so you invent all sorts of logics and reasons in order to prove them wrong. You indulge in one-upmanship, trying to bring them down or to put down their concept or theory. As an example, when you hear about the possibility of Great Eastern Sun vision—of indestructible wakefulness and fearlessness—you get freaked out. You feel jealous and envious. Because you feel so rugged and primitive, you are afraid that you might be excluded from that vision, so you stick to your particular logic, your jumbled-up confusion, your poverty mentality.

Number nine is deliberately *hoping to create harm* or having bad feelings about somebody. You don't feel good about someone, and you wish that something will go wrong for him or her. Because of the tremendous influence of theism, particularly of Christian morality, you might say that you would never think ill of anyone or wish anyone harm, that you don't even have any enemies. You could deceive other people quite easily in this regard. However, if you look at yourself very closely, you will begin to find that, in fact, you do have some kind of ill will. It might be just the slightest tinge, but you do have aggression, resentment, or hatred toward somebody.

The last of the ten evil acts is disbelieving in truth or *disbelieving in sacredness*. You refuse to work with the sense of reverence. This might make you feel like sitting on the shrine, tearing down sacred objects, or stepping on sutras, the words of the dharma. But there is something more than that. You feel totally, utterly disgusted with anything that might add new meaning to life—a sense of holiness, richness, or sacredness. You relate with meditation practice as a way of just hanging out, and chanting as just chatter. In fact, anything that you do deliberately, anything that constitutes mindfulness, is regarded as a hassle. It all boils down to an excessive casualness, not relating with yourself as having dignity or confidence. The only thing that matters to you is to stay alive—to have a roof over your head and food to eat. You simply don't believe in fundamental dignity. You believe in the wretchedness of the world rather than the sacredness of the world.

Meritorious Karma

Next we have the ten meritorious deeds of karma. Although they are meritorious, you should still regard all of them as producing further suffering, further karma. Whether you act virtuously or whether you act in a degraded manner, you are still producing pain and suffering. This continues until you realize the alternative, until you grab the other end of the stick.

The ten meritorious deeds are very simple: they are the reverse of the ten evil acts. Instead of taking life, for instance, you develop *respect for life*. Instead of stealing, you practice *generosity*. In your sexual conduct, you practice *sexual wholesomeness* and friendship. Instead of telling lies, you practice *truthfulness* and develop wholesome speech. Instead of intrigue, you practice *straightforwardness*. Instead of harsh words, you practice *good wisdom*. Instead of useless speech or gossip, you develop *simplicity*: you speak very simply, and what you say is meaningful.

Instead of wishful thinking and greediness, you have a sense of *openness*. Instead of destructive thoughts and bad feelings, you practice *gentleness*. Instead of disbelieving in sacredness, you commit yourself to understanding *sacredness*.

The general notion of karma is that a sense of uncertainty, delusion, or ignorance begins to trigger the mechanisms of lust, or passion, and aggression, which then produce karmic consequences.[3] These consequences are divided into six sections, which represent six ways of organizing our world very badly: (1) the power of volitional action, (2) experiencing what you have planted, (3) white karmic consequences, (4) changing the karmic flow by forceful action, (5) shared karmic situations, and (6) interaction of intention and action. It is quite predictable: since our world is created from passion, aggression, and ignorance, we get back from it what we have put in. Things are happening constantly in that way. It is very steady and very predictable.

1. The Power of Volitional Action

The first type of karmic consequence, known as the power of volitional action, has four subcategories.

GOOD BEGINNING, BAD ENDING. The first subcategory is good beginning, bad ending. Although the overall karmic situation you enter into might be virtuous, the result is bad. The traditional analogy is that you are born as a human being endowed with intelligence and wakefulness, or potential wakefulness; but you are born into bad circumstances. For instance, you may be poor, so although you have great intelligence, there is no freedom to practice and study because you have to keep struggling with your life. Being poor is not regarded as wicked, but it creates unreasonable obstacles for you and all sorts of extra demands, hassles, and pains—and if you are not resourceful, you remain stuck in your own poverty.

BAD BEGINNING, GOOD ENDING. In this second category, although your karmic circumstances might be bad, you receive a good ending. This is likened to being born in a rich family of *nagas* (serpentlike deities), which we could retranslate as being born in a Mafia family. It is a bad karmic situation to be born into a Mafia family. However, although your life may be leading you toward destruction, within such a family you have richness and resourcefulness, and the possibility of doing all sorts of good things. So this subcategory is quite the opposite of the previous subcategory.

BAD BEGINNING, BAD ENDING. In the third subcategory, your volitional action and what you receive from your volitional action are both bad. This is like being born into hellish circumstances and being forced to remain in that bad situation.

GOOD BEGINNING, GOOD ENDING. In the fourth category, your volitional action is good, and what you receive is also good. This is like being born as a *chakravartin*, or "universal monarch." You have the opportunity to do all sorts of things because the situation is very congenial to you.

2. Experiencing What You Have Planted

The second type of karmic consequence, experiencing what you have planted in your karmic situation, is divided into three subcategories. The first is experiencing your karmic results *immediately.* When you begin to act aggressively with anger, passion, and ignorance, then automatically, on the spot, you get your results. It is like having a fight with someone, then driving off and ending up in a car crash. It is very immediate.

In the second subcategory, the karmic consequences are experienced *later;* they do not hit you until your next birth. In the third subcategory, you experience the karmic consequences *ripening from a previous birth.* As an example, you are born in the world with an opportune situation, but somebody else comes along and disrupts that for you. You could say that this is like being born in Tibet, then getting chased out by the Communists, and ending up working in a gas station in America.

3. White Karmic Consequences

The third major type of karmic consequence, white karmic consequences, refers to good karmic situations that are perpetually growing. It has three subcategories. The first is *emulating the three jewels*—the Buddha, dharma, and sangha. You continuously get good karmic results out of that, naturally and perpetually.

The second subcategory is *emulating and appreciating somebody else's virtue*. That also leads to good karmic results and a well-favored situation. When you are inspired by somebody's wakefulness, you become wakeful as well. That is the virtue of influence.

The third subcategory is *practicing the dharma*. Even though your mind might be wandering, you are still practicing the dharma. So you have a good karmic situation in spite of the wandering of your mind.[4]

4. Changing the Karmic Flow by Forceful Action

The fourth karmic consequence is that although currently you have ended up with a very bad situation, you can suddenly change the karmic flow with a tremendous, quite sudden and forceful effort. You may have ended up in a tremendous depression, but you are able to make a jump in your life and overcome that. You are able to change the flow of your particular lifestyle. You might be used to being very lazy and sloppy, but sitting practice could tighten up your lifestyle so that suddenly you become a tidy, vigorous, and uplifting person.

There are second thoughts happening each time you act. There is hesitation, and from that hesitation or gap, you can go backward or forward. Changing the flow of karma happens in that gap. So the gap is very useful. It is in the gap that you give birth to a new life.

5. Shared Karmic Situations

The fifth karmic consequence, shared karmic situations, falls into two subcategories, national and individual karma.

NATIONAL KARMA. The first subcategory is national karma. For instance, you may be born in a particular country where you always have to relate with 7-Elevens, take-out pizza, and badly made cars. You end up in certain environments or worlds, but you cannot totally blame that on yourself. The whole country is made up that way.

INDIVIDUAL KARMA WITHIN NATIONAL KARMA. The second subcategory is individual karma within national karma. For example, if the sewage system in your neighborhood is not good, that karma is particularly and personally yours, in a sense, because the pipes keep breaking and costing you a lot of money and effort. Another example is winding up with a bad teacher who gets very grumpy because he is poorly paid by the school system. On one hand, that situation is not your fault; but on the other hand, you did end up in that particular school. You have a television network, but you have your own personal TV with which to tune in, and you also choose your own particular station. It's very simple. Environmental and individual karma complement each other; they feed each other.

6. Interaction of Intention and Action

The sixth and final karmic consequence is the interaction of intention and action. It is divided into four subcategories.

WHITE INTENTION, WHITE ACTION. The first subcategory is called completely white. An example of completely white karma is respecting your teacher and having devotion. Because that whole approach is related with healthiness rather than revolutionary thinking, ill will, and resentment, a lot of goodness comes out of it. So perpetual whiteness is created.

BLACK INTENTION, BLACK ACTION. The next subcategory is completely black. This is like taking somebody's life without any particular excuse or motivation. You have murdered somebody or destroyed something. That is completely black.

WHITE INTENTION, BLACK ACTION. The third and fourth subcategories are mixtures of white and black. The third subcategory is basically positive: with the good intention of protecting the whole, you perform a black action. For instance, with the good intention of protecting the lives of hundreds of people, you kill one person. That seems to be a good karmic situation. If somebody is going to press the button of the atomic bomb, you shoot that person. Here, the intention is white, but the action itself is black, although it has a positive effect.

BLACK INTENTION, WHITE ACTION. In the fourth subcategory, the intention is black and the action is white. This is like being very generous to your enemy while you are trying to poison him; it is a mixture of black and white.

Although people are not generally one hundred percent sane, they are worthy of our respect for their partial goodness. It's the same as saying that we can't expect perfect weather. Instead we have to expect the occasional sunshine of goodness, in spite of the snow. All six types of karmic consequences are arrived at partly due to your being in a wrong environment and partly due to your own neurosis. It is our intention to avoid such karmic consequences. However, once those two conditions come together, it is very hard to push against them. The only way to do so is by rousing the personal inspiration to try to change one's national and domestic karma.

To review, the origin of suffering is divided into two main sections: the künjung of kleshas and the künjung of karma. It seems to be quite simple: The künjung of kleshas consists of the six root kleshas, followed by the twenty subsidiary kleshas. The künjung of karma includes unmeritorious karma and meritor-ious karma (which are subdivided into three sections—body, speech, and mind), plus karmic consequences.

In hinayana, in order to cut the root of samsara, the strategy is to unplug or disconnect everything. We could actually unplug the refrigerator of samsara. It might take several hours to defrost; nevertheless, as long as we have unplugged that particular refrigerator, defrosting is going to happen. So we shouldn't feel that we are stuck with those karmic situations. We should feel that we always have the opportunity to interrupt the flow of karma. First we have to interrupt our ignorance, and second we also have to interrupt our passion. By interrupting both our ignorance and our passion, we have nothing happening in terms of the samsaric world. We have already unplugged the refrigerator.

The Truth of Cessation

The goal should be attained

CHAPTER 6

Awakening and Blossoming

It is possible to experience a moment of nirvana, a glimpse of cessation. That is what Buddha taught in his first sermon in Sarnath, when he delivered the teaching of the four noble truths, repeated four times. The Buddha said that suffering should be known; the origin of suffering should be renounced; the cessation of suffering should be realized; and the path should be regarded as the truth to resolution.

THE THIRD NOBLE TRUTH is the truth of cessation. The truth of cessation (*gokpa*) is related to the concept of *tharpa*, or "liberation." In discussing the possibility of cessation, we should get rid of fictitious stories about how great it is to get there and become somebody at last. Such ideas may be obstacles. In relating to cessation, the question is whether we have to use our imagination or whether we actually can experience a sense of relief or freedom. The truth of the matter is, that in regard to cessation, imagination does not play a very important role. It does not help at all in getting results.

The experience of cessation is very personal and very real, like the practice of meditation. Generally, however, our experiences of freedom or liberation are quite sparse and minute—and when we do have an occasional glimpse of freedom, we try to catch it, so we lose it. But it is possible to extend such glimpses. For example, if somebody is waking for the first time from a deep sleep, she might see the midnight stars. But if she waits long enough without going back to sleep, she will begin to see not only stars but the dawn, then the sunrise, and then the whole landscape being lit by a brilliant light coming from the sky. She will begin to see her hands, her palms, her toes, and she will also begin to see her tables, her chairs, and the world around her. And if she is clever enough to look at a mirror, she will also see herself.

The truth of cessation is a personal discovery. It is not mystical and it does not have any connotations of religion or psychology, it is simply your experience. If you spill boiling water on your hand, it is a personal experience: you get hurt. For that matter, if you have an orgasm, it is your personal experience: nobody else experiences it. Likewise, cessation is not just a theoretical discovery but an experience that is very real to you—a sudden gain. It is like experiencing instantaneous good health: you have no cold, no flu, no aches, and no pains in your body. You feel perfectly well, absolutely refreshed and wakeful! Such an experience is possible. Based on the fact that somebody in the past has already experienced it, you too will experience it sooner or later—although there is no guarantee, of course.

The person who has already experienced the cessation of suffering is the Buddha. The Sanskrit word *buddha* is translated into Tibetan as *sang-gye. Sang* means "awake," and *gye* means "expansion," or "blossoming." The word *sang* is related with awakening from the sleep of pain; and within the pain, suffering, and unawareness, *gye* is like a blossoming flower. Since you are awake, you collect bundles of knowledge. The knowable has become known to you through awareness and mindfulness.

From the viewpoint of the four noble truths, what we are trying to do is to become sang-gye. We are trying to blossom. We're trying to be wakeful. That is precisely what we are doing. Quite possibly we have a glimpse of sang-gye happening endlessly. Although we may think that we are fooling ourselves—and sometimes we *are* fooling ourselves—that element takes place constantly. According to the third noble truth, cessation is possible. On the path of the four noble truths we are trying to become buddhas, real buddhas, real sang-gyes.

The main obstacle to becoming buddha is samsara. The Tibetan word for samsara is khorwa: khor means "spinning" or "circulating," so khorwa means "to spin," or "those who are spinning around." Khorwa, or samsara, is equated with the ocean, because the ocean continually circulates around the world: it comes in, goes back out, comes back in, et cetera. Similarly, samsara is endless circulation. The samsaric ocean is based on three categories: the seed, the cause, and the result.

The Three Categories of Samsara

1. The Seed of Samsara: Bewilderment

The seed of samsara is the complete opposite of buddha, or awakening from suffering: it is ignorance, stupidity, basic bewilderment. Bewilderment is a psychological state that we all experience; it includes the dream state and the sleep state. Due to bewilderment, we are constantly drifting around, not knowing exactly what is happening—which is the opposite of awareness. Not seeing, not knowing, not experiencing what is happening, constantly drifting—that is the seed of samsara.

2. The Cause of Samsara: Fixation

The second category of samsara is the cause. The cause is holding on to vague concepts. That is what is called "fixation," or in Tibetan, *dzinpa. Dzin* means "to hold," so *dzinpa* means "fixation," or "grasping." Since we do not have clear perception, we must hang on to vagueness and uncertainty. In doing so, we begin to behave like a Ping-Pong ball, which does not possess any intelligence but only follows the directions of the paddle. We are bounced back and forth like a Ping-Pong ball by our fixation.

We would like to express ourselves if we feel we are undermined or if we are not acknowledged—we would like to stick our neck out—but again we are Ping-Ponged. Sometimes we feel we have so much responsibility that we would like to retire and fade away, but again we become a Ping-Pong ball. Whatever we do, our actions are not perfectly right because, based on this neurotic game, we keep being Ping-Ponged. Although it may appear that the Ping-Pong ball is commanding the players, although it seems amazing that such a little ball has so much power to direct the players' actions and even draw spectators to watch it going back and forth—actually, that is not true. The Ping-Pong ball is just a ball. It does not have any intelligence; it's just operating on reflex.

3. The Effect of Samsara: Suffering

Finally, we come to the effect. The seed of samsara is bewilderment; the cause of samsara is fixation; the effect is suffering. Since you have been constantly bounced back and forth, you begin to experience dizziness. As the Ping-Pong ball, you feel very dizzy and you ache all over your body because you've been bounced back and forth so much. The sense of pain is enormous. That is the definition of samsara.

According to the third noble truth, what we are doing is preventing, or causing the cessation of, samsara by behaving like sang-gye, or a buddha. It seems that the only way we could identify ourselves with even a pinch of the experience of buddhahood is through the experience of awareness and mindfulness practice. That is the message. At this point, cessation is not regarded as pure cessation or the complete answer—it is the message that it is possible. It is possible to develop understanding. It is possible to undo the mythical, fictional aspect of cessation and experience a glimpse of cessation as a reality, although it may be only a very short, small glimpse.

The first step is to realize you are in the samsaric mess. Although many people have heard this for years, they still do not actually *recognize* that they are being Ping-Pong-balled. That is precisely why you are in samsara—because you know what you are doing, but you still keep doing it. However, in being a Ping-Pong ball there are still gaps of *not* being one. There are gaps in which something else is experienced. In fact, during that Ping-Pong-balling, another experience takes place constantly: the experience of awareness. You begin to realize what you are, who you are, and what you are doing. But that realization could lead to spiritual materialism, which is another form of fixation— you are being Ping-Pong-balled by spirituality. However, you also realize that if there is no speed, then there is no fixation; therefore, you can transcend spiritual materialism.

A person experiences a glimpse of cessation as a kind of appetizer. If the appetizer is good, you have a sense of how the main course will be. The basic point is to *experience* cessation rather than to have a theory or a dream about it. As several contemplative gurus in the lineage have warned, too much description of the outcome is an obstacle to the path. Teachings should be based purely on the level of workability and direct personal experience. So we are following that recommendation. However, in the context of practice, as long as the approach is free from samsara, hearing descriptions of the details of the path is not particularly problematic. We could develop a very detailed and precise understanding of the nature of the path based on the process of coming back to mindfulness and awareness.

The contrast to samsara is nirvana, or peace. At this point, however, we don't have anything but samsara and little points of light that rise from the midst of darkness. Our first alternative to samsara is the practice of awareness or mindfulness, which brings us through the journey of the four noble truths. That seems to be the only way. We have to come back to becoming like Buddha. The third noble truth is very simple: nirvana is possible. Before you have complete cessation, you have to have the message that it is *possible* to have complete cessation. That message is like seeing a star in the middle of the sky on a new-moon night. Eventually, you are inspired by the crescent moon, the full moon, and then by the dawn—and finally you are inspired by the whole thing.

It is possible to experience a moment of nirvana, a glimpse of cessation. That is what Buddha taught in his first sermon in Sarnath, when he delivered the teaching of the four noble truths, repeated four times. The Buddha said that cessation could be experienced. He said that suffering should be known; the origin of suffering should be renounced; the cessation of suffering should be realized; and the path should be regarded as the truth to resolution. That's almost word for word.

CHAPTER 7

Meditation as the Path to Buddhahood

The path of meditation leads to shinjang, *being thoroughly processed or trained, which is the result or achievement of shamatha-vipashyana meditation. Although you may not have experienced the final development yet, it is no big secret that there is a final development. You can't pretend that the Buddha didn't exist and still talk about his teachings, because he actually did it—he achieved enlightenment. We can't keep that a secret.*

THE THIRD NOBLE TRUTH is based on recognizing the contrast between samsara and nirvana. In the technique of meditating on the breathing, there is automatically and naturally such a contrast. You realize that something is alternating in you, that your sanity and your insanity are alternating. You experience a gap. Relating to that gap is relating to the contrast between samsara and nirvana.

The traditional analogy for the cessation of suffering is the blowing out of a candle. This refers to the final stage of cessation, when you have become buddha. But effort and energy is required even to get to the *idea* of blowing out the candle. You first need to realize that the candle is not all that powerful, that it is feeble, so you could actually blow it out. Once you realize you can blow out the candle, even at a distance, you have gotten the message. And when that message is a reality, blowing out the candle becomes simply a matter of effort.

The cessation of samsara happens when you act like Buddha. The Buddha was just one person, however. The liberated state of mind could be different, or have a different style, for each individual. What we are concerned with now, however, is training. Once you have been trained, you might exercise that training in your own particular way. For example, after you pass the driver's test, which is the same for everyone, you might drive differently than other people who passed the test. In the vajrayana, or tantra, the different levels and styles that people operate with are categorized. But as far as hinayana is concerned, it is simply a question of experiencing basic liberation.

Attaining liberation takes work. It is like making jewelry. When you go to a jeweler, he has solid gold, solid silver, or solid brass lumps hanging around that are ugly and don't look particularly ornamental. But when you ask him to make a ring or a necklace or some earrings, he gets out a lump and begins to make something out of it, and it becomes a beautiful thing. Likewise, when you buy a car, you could remember that your newly bought automobile is not born out of a lotus; it's made in a factory. It may *seem* as if it's born out of a lotus, but that's not quite true. It is the same thing with buddhahood, which is supposed to be spotless and fantastic. To become buddha is a final inspiration; to become buddha—wow! But the Buddha did not come out of a lotus; he came out of a factory.

The cessation of suffering is connected with the fourth noble truth, which is the path, or *lam* in Tibetan. Cessation and the path work together: when there is a path, cessation automatically dawns; and when there is cessation, that allows you to follow the path. The path consists of following the example of the Buddha through the practice of meditation, through mindfulness and awareness. That practice is one of the merits of the hinayana discipline.

The reason the hinayana is known as the "lesser vehicle" is because it is straight and narrow. There isn't much room to improvise. Since there is no improvisation, we can develop what is known as individual salvation. Individual salvation is not a selfish goal; it is self-discipline, straight and simple. It is simple in the sense that there is not much to do other than just fully being there. The path of meditation leads to *shinjang*, being thoroughly processed or trained, which is the result or achievement of shamatha-vipashyana meditation. Although you may not have experienced the final development yet, it is no big secret that there is a final development. You can't pretend that the Buddha didn't exist and still talk about his teachings, because he actually did it—he achieved enlightenment. We can't keep that a secret. In the meantime, however, you could regard any sense of promise that comes into your mind, any hope that comes up, as another thought. If there is a strong desire to achieve a result, that will push you back. You could relate to hope as respect for the dharma, or the truth, rather than a promise. It is like a schoolchild seeing a professor: one day she too might become a professor, but she still has to do her homework. Similarly, particularly in the hinayana, there is a journey going on all the time.

Shinjang happens in stages. It begins with the achievement of clarity. This level is like seeing one glimpse of what it would be like if you had that glimpse constantly. In order to achieve permanent cessation, you have to continue with the practice. So first you have a glimpse, which is like the appetizer; then that appetizer makes you hungrier. You want to have a big meal; therefore, you are willing to wait, maybe hours and hours, for the big meal to come.

When you develop shinjang, the sense of turmoil and misery subsides. Therefore, both physically and mentally, there is a feeling of comfort. Comfort does not mean euphoria, but the sense that things are soothing because you have simplified your life. Simplicity brings tremendous relief. Nonetheless, you don't look for final results and you do not become goal-oriented; you just keep on practicing. Having practiced enough, achievement comes naturally. If you are constantly trying to achieve cessation, it is a problem—you will not achieve it in that way. Whenever you take an ego-oriented approach, you become allergic to yourself. There is no other way but to step out of that. So attaining individual salvation does not come from seeking salvation— salvation simply dawns.

Cessation and salvation come to you as you become a reasonable person. You become reasonable and meticulous because you cease to be sloppy and careless. Therefore, there is a sense of relief. Meticulousness is exemplified by *oryoki* practice, a formal style of serving and eating food that has its origins in Zen Buddhism. In this practice you are aware of everything that is being done, every move. At the same time, you are not uptight, for once you become self-conscious, you begin to forget the oryoki procedures. This logic also applies to keeping your room tidy, taking care of your clothing, taking care of your lifestyle altogether. Being meticulous is not based on fear; it is based on natural mindfulness.

As a final achievement, if you lose your mindfulness, a reminder comes back to you directly in the process of acting sloppy. Such reminders are a result of first having tremendous discipline. Because you have been with your practice constantly, reminders come up. If you have spent time with a friend, someone whom you love very much, and that friend goes away, each time you think of your friend, you develop more affection for him or her. In the same way, if you are at the more advanced level of shinjang, whenever sloppiness happens, that sloppiness itself automatically reminds you and brings you back. So a natural system of checks and balances begins to take place. In that way, you become like the Buddha. Every little detail of your life has meaning. There is a natural and dignified way to eat food and a natural and dignified way to relate with anything else that occurs in your life. Instead of your life being a situation of suffering, it becomes soothing. That is why shamatha is known as the development of peace. Peace does not mean pleasure seeking, but harmony. You don't create chaos for yourself or for others, and you start by first working with yourself.

Traditionally, there are four ways of taking care of your body and developing wholesomeness. The first way is relating properly to food. As in oryoki practice, you don't consume large amounts of food, nor do you eat too little. Rather, you eat enough to leave some room in your stomach. The second way is relating properly to sleep or rest. You don't push yourself constantly, but you learn how to rest. Resting in this way is different from resting in the ordinary sense, where you are sometimes still working hard.

The third way is taking care of details, which means physically taking care of yourself: taking care of your body, taking care of your clothing, taking care of your environment. How you move physically, how you handle things, is more important than simply how you appear. Beyond mere appearance, there is a quality of meticulousness. The fourth way is meditation: without that reference point, there would be no real relief or wholesomeness. So food, sleep, taking care of your well-being, and meditation are the four ways to develop wholesomeness; and such wholesomeness leads you to develop the state of individual salvation. That is why it is said that the dharma is good at the beginning, good in the middle, and good at the end.

In working with yourself, you start with the outer form; then that outer form brings an inner feeling; and finally that inner feeling brings a deeper sense of freedom. So it is a threefold process. This same process could apply to anything you do. In the beginning, it is mostly a big hassle; in the middle, it is sometimes a hassle and sometimes it is natural; then finally it becomes natural. With sitting practice as well: first it is a struggle; at some stage it is both a struggle and a relief; and finally, it is very easy. It's like putting on a new ring: for the first few days it feels like it is in the way; but eventually it becomes a part of your hand. It is that kind of logic. As for myself, since the age of five I was raised in an environment of constant discipline. If I lost my awareness, I would be reminded by my tutor or by my disciplinarian, not just by myself, so by now it seems to have become natural. It's not that I myself have achieved a great thing, particularly; but it is thanks to my disciplinarian and my teacher.

CHAPTER 8

Transcending Samsara and Nirvana

The idea of cessation is transcending the turmoil and problems of life and the neurosis that goes along with them. However, because we try so hard to transcend all that, we are unable to do so. The very fact of trying so hard is the way we got into trouble in the first place. So in regard to cessation, definitely the most important point is that it transcends both samsara and nirvana. By transcending both samsaric and nirvanic possibilities of confusion, we are transcending cessation itself, so there is no ground. But that groundlessness itself could become a very powerful expression of cessation.

FROM THE HINAYANA point of view, cessation means being able to prevent problems or use them up. The Sanskrit word for cessation is *nirodha*, and in Tibetan, it is *gokpa*, which in verb form means "to stop" or "to prevent." The idea of cessation is not so much being calmed down as suddenly being stopped. Sometimes *gokpa* refers to the final goal, the state of enlightenment, or freedom. However, in this case, gokpa is not regarded as the final goal; instead, it simply means that temporarily problems have been prevented. We have been able to cut through them, to cut them down. Having cut unnecessary garbage, we are able to develop real living sanity and to let that shine through. Cessation refers to the prevention of unnecessary hassle; however, a level of hassle still remains. It is like having nice food and being satisfied with your particular dish, but still having the hassle that you have to pay for it.

Gokpa also refers to the final goal, the state of enlightenment or freedom. Gokpa has the quality of a vaccination: once problems are prevented, it is for good. Cessation means that we are actually able to prevent karmic chain reactions as well as karmic consequences on the spot. That possibility comes from our own realization and experience of the journey. We begin to feel that we could prevent such problems by being highly disciplined and by having a genuine connection with our own mind and thought patterns, which could be good or bad, virtuous or otherwise. The question is how to unplug, how to switch off the electricity without getting a shock. As far as shamatha practice is concerned, the way to do so is by nonparticipation in the samsaric world. You become a monk or a nun. You become a good practitioner who sits a lot, for during sitting practice you are preventing karma, or at least you are not committing any wrong-doings. That logic might seem simpleminded, but it is not simply that if you don't do anything, that is good, and if you do lots of things, that is bad. The logic is that when you are meditating, you are actually boycotting the process of furthering anything at all.

There are various degrees of cessation. There could be a lesser, medium, or greater degree of cessation. Because we understand how cessation evolves, we begin to feel that we are actually making progress. We develop a sense of friendliness, ease, and self-respect. We have fewer complaints and less resentment. We can look at ourselves in the mirror and see how much we have changed from when we first started to practice. We see that we have developed a sense of confidence and genuineness. Basically, we see that we used to eat garbage and now we are beginning to change our diet; and we realize that we would never do that again. Those very simple things are signs of nirodha.

Although you begin to recognize those signs of cessation, at the same time, you don't need to hang on to such signs. You don't need confirmation or reassurance; you just keep going. Looking for reassurance would be returning to künjung, the origin of suffering, and you don't want to do that. One experience of pain is good enough. The fascination that drives you back to pain no longer applies. Would you put your finger on an electric burner when it is burning hot, if you had done that once already? Obviously not. Likewise, once you have realized the truth of suffering and the origin of suffering fully and properly, you never make the same mistake again. This happens by instinct, as well as by studying and practicing. The mahayanists would say that everyone possesses the nature of wakefulness, called *tathagatagarbha*, or buddha nature, which forces you to see through your pain and make sure that it is not repeated.

Experientially, cessation means that thoughts become transparent. Thoughts are no longer a big hassle in sitting practice. With cessation, such thoughts become too absurd to occur. Experiencing the transparency of thoughts seems to depend on the long-range discipline of the student. During sitting practice, very powerful thoughts take place. We get angry with this and that—my this and my that, other people's this's and that's. There are occasional punctuations of wondering what kind of food we are going to eat, whether we have to take a shower and buy some shampoo. All sorts of thoughts, both little thoughts and powerful thoughts, occasionally take place, but all of those thoughts are seen to be transparent rather than solid. Cessation occurs when there is no implication behind such thoughts—they are just ripples in the pond.

The Twelve Aspects of Cessation

Traditionally, the discussion of cessation is divided into twelve topics. In *The Treasury of Knowledge*, Jamgön Kongtrül also listed these twelve topics.

1. Nature

The first topic is the nature of cessation, which has three categories: the origin, what to give up, and what to cultivate.

THE ORIGIN: MEDITATIVE ABSORPTION. The origin of cessation is meditative absorption, a pure state of mind beyond ignorance. You begin to understand the nature of reality by developing meditative absorption through the practice of shamatha discipline, which reduces kleshas.

WHAT SHOULD BE GIVEN UP: NEUROSIS. What should be given up, overlooked, or transcended is neurosis. Through mindfulness and awareness, you experience the possibility of not committing yourself to the kleshas. You are beginning to develop a sense of goodness and toughness, which automatically prevents you from being sloppy.

THE PATH TO BE CULTIVATED: SIMPLICITY. What should be cultivated is simplicity. Simplicity means that you keep everything to a minimum. You keep your life very simple: you could get up, practice, eat breakfast, go to work, come back, have dinner, practice again, and go to sleep. Ideally, good practitioners are supposed to sandwich their lives between morning and evening meditation practice. This simplifies things and cuts through unnecessary entertainment. In terms of sitting, you don't create any conditions at all, such as asking, "Should I sit in the morning? Should I sit in the evening?" There is no question about it. You are totally and completely influenced by your shamatha practice and by the simplicity of your involvement with the buddhadharma.

Fundamentally, the nature of cessation is based on a pure state of mind. Having overcome or seen through the temporary obstacles or veils that prevent us from seeing things as they are—seeing properly with clear vision—there are no further difficulties. Having overcome our inability to relate with our basic nature, nothing needs to be prevented and nothing needs to be cultivated. The obstacles covering our basic sanity are not regarded as hardened, as fastened on with powerful glue or difficult to remove, but as detachable. It is like removing clouds in order to see the sun. Nonetheless, it can be hard to see things that way.

2. Profundity

The second topic is profundity. Profundity means developing subtleness in your attitude toward cessation, understanding that cessation is nobody's property. Cessation does not come from elsewhere, it is part of you; and at the same time, seemingly, it is not particularly a part of you. Basically, what is part of you and what is not part of you are always questionable. Cessation cannot be regarded as the product of either your personal effort or someone else's suggestion. So, as a practitioner, you should not take pride in your effort or feel arrogant, thinking that you have brought about the cessation of the samsaric world. It is not *your* cessation—at the same time, cessation does not belong to others.

You practice due to your own inspiration. Nobody can make you do it if you don't want to. You do not have to depend on local deities or national deities or religious sectarian deities. Such inspiration seems to be a natural part of you; but, in fact, the path is not part of your basic system, because it is foreign to your usual style of thinking, which is neurosis. There is a problem when your inspiration develops into a sense that knowledge and you are completely one, for if you have a sense of complete "oneness," there is no urge to follow any discipline, such as the hinayana discipline of creating no harm. That kind of discipline seems to lose the quality of naturalness.

Somebody presenting the language of sanity to you is using a different kind of logic than the habitual logic of neurosis, however philosophical and natural it may seem. At the same time, you cannot ignore the fact that basic sanity exists naturally in your state of being, and that through discipline you are able to understand both the origin and the cessation of suffering. So if you ask whether the path is part of your basic system or not, the answer is that it is both.

Dharma is based on a sense of separation in that foreign information is coming to you. However, when that information cannot be properly and fully absorbed or digested, and you continue to regard it as separate, you have a problem. It is also problematic if you try to maintain your particular territory by picking and choosing what has been given to you. On one hand, there is no difference between dharma, discipline, and yourself: dharma is an expression of yourself. On the other hand, if you think there is no difference between you and the dharma, so you can make up your own dharma as you go along, that is not quite the case. You have inherited examples of the dharma through a lineage, and you have to follow such examples. You can't be that freestyle.

The dharma is not absolutely everything and it is not absolutely nothing—it is both. It is not even both, and it is absolutely not neither. Dharma is not yours and it is not others'. Dharma is both yours and others'. At the same time, dharma is not made out of both you and others jumbled together, like a sweet and sour dish. Therefore, you and the dharma are not one, nor are you and the dharma completely separate. So what do we finally have? Very little, or quite a lot. The only possibility is that at one and the same time, the simplicity of the practice can be developed with respect to the tradition and discipline, and your intuition can be developed according to your own basic understanding of life. That is the point of profundity.

3. Sign

The third topic is sign. The sign that you have achieved cessation, or gokpa, is that the kleshas have begun to subside. Little by little, you find that they gradually cease to exist. You begin to become somewhat bland, ordinary, and boring. Because of your practice, you cease to play games and you become a decent person. You are cleaned up, so to speak, and you become a more reasonable person—on the spot, or gradually. The ultimate sign is realizing that there are no more hang-ups of any kind. At that point, you have achieved nirodha and begun to experience nirvana.

Sign or token means that you are giving up worldly commitments in the sense of pure, unreasonable indulgence. Even sensible worldly people would not regard such indulgence as good. Beyond that, you are becoming highly disciplined. You are realistic, proper, and industrious; you have self-discipline and project dignity. Such ordinary decency is recognized as a token of cessation. There is virtue in such everyday logic as driving carefully and not bouncing your checks. Although those virtues may seem superficial, little things like that are still considered to be related with the possibility of gokpa. That is, the logic of ordinary household life is directed toward cessation: there is an element of sanity and of transcending samsara. Although that may seem like a vague possibility, such logic has juice in it, and truth.

4. Ultimate

The fourth topic is ultimate. It is based on applying the understanding and discipline of *prajna,* or knowledge, in our approach to life. Through prajna we begin to realize the origin of our problems and our mistakes, which occur from ignorance. We develop a real understanding of where the confusion and chaos take place. Having understood that, there is no possibility of regressing. From this point of view, our journey could be considered a one-shot deal. It is never regarded as purely a rehearsal.

Through the practice of shamatha, you begin to develop "noble prajna"—supreme prajna that transcends the ordinary world. You realize on an intellectual level how and why suffering and the origin of suffering can be overcome. You develop a genuine understanding of how things work. In other words, you don't panic. When you panic, you lose sight of noble prajna. You just beat around the bush, asking, "How should I be doing this? Why should I be doing this?" You become a beggar of incompetency. But with noble prajna, you become confident. You begin to see the value of the intellect, which in this case means sharpened clarity rather than theory. Instead of resorting to Jungian or Freudian styles of psychologizing everything, you are simply experiencing your life and understanding how it works. In the experience of prajna, you know what to do and how to do it properly and fully. Through intellect, you are able to overcome what should be avoided: the seed, or origin, of suffering.

5. Incompletion

The fifth topic is incompletion. When you reach a certain level of spiritual achievement, or cessation, you begin to understand that although you have been able to reach that level, things are not properly completed. You understand that although you have overcome problems and obstacles, you have not yet blossomed. The student of hinayana who first enters the discipline is known as a *stream-winner.* Having entered into the system of discipline, you have overcome the hang-up against clear seeing, seeing things as they are. But once you join the path of clear seeing, you find that along with that, there are further hang-ups. There are also students who have reached the level known as *once-returner,* meaning that you only return to the world for one more lifetime, you do not keep returning due to karmic debts. Although you have not completely overcome the world of pleasure and passion, or completely clarified the world of desire, and therefore still have problems; you are still regarded as a person who has achieved a kind of liberation or salvation. Even for those who in their next life do not return to the world of samsara, people called *nonreturners,* the attainment of gokpa is still incomplete or temporary. All such students are partially delivered and partially confused; nonetheless, their incomplete cessation could still be called a form of salvation.

6. Signs of Completion

The sixth topic is signs of completion. At this point you have become an arhat, somebody who has completely overcome or controlled any obstacles to the path. Arhats have already restrained what should be restrained and developed what should be developed. Your learning is completely accomplished and you have reached a state of nonlearning. However, this state of no more learning refers purely to the arhats on the hinayana level, rather than to the bodhisattva or the buddha level. It refers to arhats who have reached the state of no more learning as far as their own particular arhatship world is concerned. It has nothing to do with the five paths in vajrayana, in which the path of no more learning would be buddhahood.[1]

To review, in the hinayana there are stream-winners, once-returners, nonreturners, and arhats. When students first enter the path, they are called stream-winners. Since stream-winners and once-returners emphasize meditative absorptions, *dhyanas* (or *jhanas*),[2] they remain within the realm of passion. Nonreturners are able to conquer the realm of passion, but they are still working with samsaric mind and with the Hindu notion of attaining divine achievement. They continue to work with that until they become complete arhats, when finally they cut the whole thing. Nonreturners are incomplete because they are still in the process of not returning. (I think Nagarjuna would like that particular wit.)[3]

Arhats progress through the four jhana states, or meditative absorptions, and beyond. Nobody knows exactly what happens at that point; there is a lot of philosophical disagreement about that. In my school,[4] we take the position that when somebody is able to completely overcome the four jhana states and the four formless jhana states, he or she becomes a real Buddhist rather than wandering in samsara. In other words, because the jhana states are still involved in samsaric possibilities, such meditative absorptions should be transcended.

7. Without Ornament

The seventh aspect of gokpa is without ornament, without embellishment. At this stage, although you have developed prajna, which has led you to fully overcome conflicting emotions, you are not adorned with any signs of holiness or dignity. You have accomplished much on a personal level, but you do not manifest that to the rest of the world. Some texts would call this being unable to perform miracles, which is a somewhat questionable subject. We could refer to miracles more as a sense of real command over the world. Basically, "without ornament" means that you are not ready to be a teacher, although you have developed yourself thoroughly and fully. You may have transcended neurotic hang-ups, but you are still unable to manifest to students, to yourself, and to the world as a highly accomplished person. So you are unadorned as a teacher.

8. Adorned

The eighth topic is adorned; it is gokpa with embellishment or ornamentation. At this point, you have become a teacher. You have developed confidence and flair, and your individual discipline has also developed. Having already overcome the veil of neurosis and the veil of karmic obligations, you have achieved power over the world.

9. With Omission

Number nine is with omission. Although you have transcended the passions and neurosis of the human realm, you are still unable to accomplish real sanity completely and properly. You have attained freedom, in knowing how to avoid being born in the hell realm, the hungry ghost realm, the animal realm, the human realm, the jealous-god realm, and part of the god realm; but the realm of the formless gods has not yet been transcended. That portion of the realm of the gods is the holiest of holy, the highest samsaric realm. This is exemplified in the Hindu religion by the striving to attain brahmahood and then to transcend it. In Hinduism, there are levels beyond brahmahood, where *brahma* (Godhead) becomes the universality of *brahman* (the Absolute).[5] In terms of Christianity, we could say that you have completed your training, but you haven't quite connected with the Godhead. Since the neurosis of an abstract notion of the ultimate has not been completely conquered, there is an omission. Even would-be arhats, would-be bodhisattvas, or would-be buddhas practicing the path of buddhadharma still have such subtle theistic hang-ups.

10. Without Omission

The tenth topic is without omission. Without omission means that you have transcended even the majestic and mystical concept of Godhead or brahmahood. You have finally conquered the whole theistic world. Here, all the neuroses and habitual patterns are transcended. However, that does not mean you are becoming a bodhisattva or a buddha. We are talking about somebody who is on the hinayana level. At this level, you have just barely managed to cope with things as they are. You have seen that the hassles of samsara are fantastically vivid and obvious, but that the hassles of nirvana are much more so. So when the hassles of nirvana are overcome, and you are actually able to become a reasonably respectable nirvanic person, it is quite a big deal. That is the definition of gokpa, or cessation, from the true hinayana point of view. You become a good citizen of hinayana, somebody who has truly attained the state of cessation.

11. Especially Supreme

The eleventh topic is known as especially supreme, or extraordinary. At this level, you have transcended both samsara and nirvana. You do not mingle in samsaric neurosis, but you have also transcended the potential of nirvanic neurosis. This topic seems to have been inserted by the mahayanists; however, since it is a part of the list accepted by Jamgön Kongtrül in his *Treasury of Knowledge*, we better go along with that. Nirvana means dwelling in peace and openness, and samsara means dwelling in one's neurosis. In achieving ultimate gokpa, especially supreme cessation, you finally have the ability to refrain from dwelling in either samsara or nirvana. This topic is tinged with mahayana; the pure hinayana version does not mention not dwelling in nirvana, since that is their goal.

12. Beyond Calculation

The twelfth topic is beyond calculation. When we actually experience cessation properly, we realize that whatever needed to be overcome has been overcome. We attain an ultimate state of peace, relaxation, and openness, in which we are no longer hassled by the samsaric world. The topic of beyond calculation includes within it several further aspects of gokpa. These definitions of gokpa are not particularly categorized, but random.

RENUNCIATION. The first definition is renunciation. Having already renounced, you have reached a state in which you do not have to try to renounce anything—you are already there. This is like somebody who has given up smoking and who has no desire at all to smoke more cigarettes, or an alcoholic who has become a teetotaler with no desire to drink. You have renounced your whatever and reached the state of gokpa.

COMPLETE PURIFICATION. The next definition is complete purification. There are no hang-ups involved in the journey of reaching the state of gokpa—everything is purified.

WORN OUT. Gokpa has also been called "worn out," or the wearing-out process. It is the wearing out of subtle neurosis and obvious neurosis, both at the same time. Everything is well worn out: it is a sort of bankruptcy of all levels of neurosis.

PASSIONLESSNESS. Gokpa is passionlessness, which is the basic definition of dharma.

CESSATION. Once we have reached the state of gokpa, since there is no desire or aggression, there is cessation. More closely, there is no desire to initiate further involvement in the samsaric world.

COMPLETE PEACE. Gokpa is complete peace, which is connected with the idea of energy. It is not that somebody is dead and we write on the dead person's tombstone that this person has gone to his final rest, as in "Rest in Peace." Buddhists have a different concept of peace than the theistic world might have. Peace is energetic; it has immense power and energy. Actually, that is the source of a sense of humor, which is also a definition of cessation.

SUBSIDING. The last definition is what is known as subsiding or setting, like the sunset. Subsiding is giving up hope, not hanging on to the possibility of sunrise. You are giving up altogether all the neuroses and problems of the previous eleven possibilities.

In looking at the view of cessation and the various definitions of gokpa, we need to know how we could use these concepts and ideas. Altogether, cessation means transcending the turmoil and problems of life and the neurosis that goes along with them. However, we try so hard to transcend all that, that we are unable to do so, because the very fact of trying so hard is the way we got into trouble in the beginning. So in regard to cessation, definitely the most important point is number eleven, "especially supreme": the transcendence of both samsara and nirvana. By transcending both samsaric and nirvanic possibilities of confusion, we are transcending cessation itself, so there is no ground. At the same time, that groundlessness itself could become a very powerful expression of cessation.

We can actually achieve cessation if we have no personal involvement in it. However, when we want to watch our own cessation, we are simply cranking up the wheel of samsara all over again, in the name of freedom. We are returning to the first and second nidanas: to ignorance and volitional action. But when we have abandoned any personal ego input, any personal bank account, we begin to achieve proper cessation. In the long run this would be our best investment, but it appears to be a very bad business deal because we don't have any legal contract to protect ourselves—we are no longer existing!

The Truth of the Path

The path should be actualized

CHAPTER 9

The Doubtless Path

*The nature of the path is more like an expedition or explor-
ation than following a road that already has been built.
When people hear that they should follow the path, they
might think that a ready-made system exists and that individual expressions are not required. They may think that one
does not actually have to surrender or give or open. But when
you actually begin to tread on the path, you realize that you
have to clear out the jungle and all the trees, underbrush,
and obstacles growing in front of you. You have to bypass
tigers and elephants and poisonous snakes.*

T HE FOURTH NOBLE TRUTH is the truth of the path. The nature of the path is up to you: it is your doing, in a sense, but
there are guidelines. A do-it-yourself kit is presented to you by
your teacher. You are given all the necessary equipment and all
the necessary attitudes; then you are sent off to the jungle and
you have to live by means of your survival kit. In the midst of
this samsaric jungle, you have to learn to survive and come out
the other side.

The Sequence of the Path

As you begin your path, you encounter impermanence, suffering,
emptiness, and egolessness as a sequential process. These could
be viewed as problems or promises, but basically, traveling on the
path, you need to know what to expect and what to overcome.

Overcoming the Notion of Eternity

The first thing to overcome is the notion of eternity. In the case of the nontheistic path of buddhadharma, looking for eternity could become problematic; so, in order to transcend the concept of eternity, we have the wisdom of impermanence. The wisdom of impermanence applies to whatever is subject to becoming, to happening, or to being gathered together. It is all very transitory.

Overcoming the Search for Pleasure

The second thing to be overcome is our constant search for pleasure. Our searching for pleasure, whether simple or complicated, is prominent and continuous. It is connected with the problem of spiritual materialism. In order to overcome that obstacle to the path, we have the slogan: "Because everything is impermanent, everything is always painful and subject to suffering."

Realizing the Possibility of Emptiness

Once there is suffering, a sense of desolation takes place as you begin to realize that both the things that exist outside you and the things that exist inside you are subject to impermanence and suffering. You realize the possibility of emptiness, a gap of nothingness—pure, plain emptiness. Things are emptyhearted and nonexistent.

Encountering Egolessness

Having realized emptiness, you also begin to realize that there is no one to hang on to that realization or to celebrate that experience. You encounter egolessness. Ego refers to the notion of self that we always feel, the sense of center. "Centering" has become a popular concept in the jargon of spirituality, but there is no mention of giving up or surrendering—it is more like having a little doggie bag inside you to hold your leftovers. The problem with centering is that you are coming back to a sense of your individual being, as opposed to a selfless center. A center that is very full, definite, solid, and concretized in that way is called ego.

Having such a solid sense of isness, you no longer have a path. But at the same time, having such a problem means that you have something to work on. However, what Buddhism is trying to tell you is that you could do your fieldwork without having any central headquarters, and you do not need to have a bureaucracy of meditative techniques. Dignity is not based on self and other, but comes from heaven down to earth—and the more you let go, the more dignity takes place.

Four Qualities of the Path

The path has been described as having four qualities: path, insight, practice, and fruition. All together, the nature of the path is more like an expedition or exploration than following a road that already has been built. When people hear that they should follow the path, they might think that a ready-made system exists and that individual expressions are not required. They may think that one does not actually have to surrender, or give, or open. But when you actually begin to tread on the path, you realize that you have to clear out the jungle and all the trees, underbrush, and obstacles growing in front of you. You have to bypass tigers and elephants and poisonous snakes.

The realization that you actually have to make your own way through this jungle of samsaric chaos may be a shock, but such a shock might be appropriate and good. If you do not have any understanding of that quality of the path, and instead feel that blessings are going to descend on you just like that, there is no point in having a path. The path would no longer be a journey. Instead, it would be like simply buying your ticket, checking yourself in, depositing your baggage, and getting your seat; then sitting and getting bored; and finally someone announcing that you are at the end of the journey already so you can get off the transport. In that approach, there is a feeling of being cheated. There is no development taking place. The path is designed both to clear out obstacles and to develop particular patterns or qualities. It is very hard work.

1. Path: Searching for the Real Meaning of Suchness

The first quality of the path is that it is, in fact, a path: it is a search for the real meaning of dharma, the real meaning of isness or suchness. However, you do not try to pinpoint the isness—and if you try *not* to pinpoint it, you are doing it already. But this is getting beyond the hinayana, becoming more Zenny. In the Buddhist-English terminology that has developed, suchness or isness refers to something that is fully and truly there. It is connected with rediscovering buddha nature.

2. Insight: Through Clarity, Transcending Neurosis

The second quality of the path is that it is a path of insight. The journey that you are going along, and the discipline that you are going through, is based on sitting meditation practice, as well the experience of day-to-day living. Both are supposed to be aids for transcending neurosis, but it seems to be necessary to put your mind and effort into it. This may seem like a somewhat goal-oriented approach, but at the hinayana level, there is no other choice. The sitting practice of meditation is based on shamatha discipline, which provides immense clarity and the ability to relate with situations very fully, precisely, and completely. Any neurosis that comes up becomes extremely visible and clear—and each time a certain neurosis arises, appropriate to the time, that neurosis itself becomes a spokesperson to develop further clarity. So a neurosis serves two purposes: showing the path and showing its own suicidal quality. That is what is known as insight, knowing the nature of dharmas as they are.

3. Practice: Associating with Basic Sanity

The third quality of the path is known as practice. Practice enables us to relate with misconceptions of the dharma, such as eternalism and nihilism. Once you are able to relate with sitting meditation, and you are familiar with that particular experience, you find that sitting practice is not an endurance contest or a way of proving who is the best boy or girl. Instead, meditation practice is about how you can become a rock or an ocean—a living rock or a living ocean.

By sitting, we can absorb a lot of things and we can reject a lot of things; nevertheless, things do not particularly change. It is a larger-scale approach to life. In ordinary situations we may think that we are so sophisticated and that we know what we are doing. In terms of our domestic life, we may feel we have everything under control. We know how to book tickets on airplanes or to hitchhike across the country, and we have all the maps figured out. However, although we may feel we have everything under control—or we may not feel that way, and wish we could—there are still a lot of loose ends. Such loose ends cannot be covered by simply running down a list. Our list becomes so large that finally we cannot handle it without more and more energy.

In contrast, in the sitting practice of meditation, you are becoming like a rock, like an ocean. You do not have to go through any list; you just *are* that way, you are just *being*. You percolate or freeze in your own way. You just *be* that way. It is not particularly rewarding, but there is a sense of satisfaction, clarity, and immense dignity. Through meditation practice, you are associating yourself with basic sanity, which takes place continuously. So practice plays a very important part.

4. Fruition: Permanent Nirvana

The fourth quality of the path is fruition. In the hinayana approach to life, fruition is the idea of a permanent nirvana. Permanent nirvana means that we have learned the lesson of neurosis and its tricks, which are played on us all the time and take advantage of our weakness. Once we have learned this lesson, it is quite likely that we will not do the same thing again. That is also the case with our habitual patterns, unless we are complete maniacs.

At this point, although we have learned our lesson, ordinary little habitual patterns are still going to pull us back over and over. Those little habits, although similar to larger-scale mistakes, are not that problematic. The idea of fruition is that we are not going to keep making large-scale mistakes—like wanting to be saved, or wanting to be blissed out, or wanting to indulge. We have learned from our mistakes, so we are not going to make the same mistake twice.

If there is a complete understanding of the nature of the path, it seems to be a doubtless path. But this does not mean that you do not question anything. Questioning is in accordance with the doubtless path; within that path, doubt is part of the methodology and questioning is necessary. One should not be too gullible. Constant suspicion is very good—it is a highlight, like a Star of David—but at the same time, the path transcends all doubts. Fruition is knowing that we finally have a direction, in spite of all the little freak-outs taking place all the time. We no longer say things like, "Well, this path is better than others, but something else might be better still and more pleasurable," because we have cut through the idea of pleasure, and we have also cut through the idea of eternity and the self-snugness of the ego. Everything has been cut through.

CHAPTER 10

The Five Paths

The path does not really exist unless you are available. It is as if you are the road worker, the surveyor, and the traveler, all at once. As you go along, the road gets built, the survey's done, and you become a traveler.

F ROM THE PRACTITIONER'S point of view, there's an interesting link between the first noble truth and the last noble truth: the first noble truth could be described as the ground on which the fourth noble truth is founded. That is, the realization of suffering brings an understanding and discovery of the path. The problem with the word *path* is that we automatically think that the road has been built and the highway is open so that we can drive nonstop. There's a possibility of taking too much comfort in having a path, thinking that since the path has already been laid down, you do not have to choose which path to take— there's simply *the* path. That attitude seems to be the product of misunderstanding or cowardliness on the part of the student. In fact, the path does not really exist unless you are available. It is as if you are the road worker, the surveyor, and the traveler, all at once. As you go along, the road gets built, the survey's done, and you become a traveler.

There is another kind of path that *has* already been built for you, which you should know about, called the "general path" or the "common path." In the general path, value judgments and morals have already been developed, such as the virtues of democracy, the idea of a good man or good woman, or the purity of the social worker—you just enlist, become a member, and go to work. The commonsense path tells you that it's nice to be polite, that good manners always work, and that kindhearted people are constantly loved. It might also include Buddhist teachings such as "Control your senses, control your mind, get to know yourself." On the common spiritual path, there is an emphasis on getting psychologically high, becoming an accomplished meditator. By concentrating on a burning candle, you could develop your concentration, attain a state of *samadhi,* and experience the One, the realm of the gods.

The common path is not as accurate or profound as the Buddhist path, but it is not by any means the object of mockery. As Buddhists, we too follow common rules and regulations. For instance, we don't shoplift, but we pay for the things we buy. However, in terms of dharma, such norms are just sidelines, not what we concentrate on. Many scriptures, and even sutras, talk about the common path as the starting point for students who are beginning at the beginning. For students who see the world in a very naive way and have naive attitudes toward spirituality, goodness is the issue, peace is the issue, euphoric states of samadhi are the issue; therefore, they try to cultivate those things. However, from the Buddhist point of view, that is dwelling in the *devaloka,* the god realm. In cultivating meditative absorptions, or jhana states, you are appreciating the advertisement rather than wholeheartedly getting into the path itself. The extraordinary thing about the Buddhist approach is that such conventionality is regarded as unnecessary. On the Buddhist path, instead of trying to cultivate the jhana states, you come directly to the mind—a mind that is developing its awareness, openness, painfulness, or whatever it may be.

The path has many stages. To begin with, it is a series of steps; then it becomes a county road, and finally a highway. At the beginning the path is just a footpath, a trail. We have to cut down and tame ourselves much more at the beginning than at the end. We have to develop a sense of renunciation. If we simply stepped out of our house into a luxurious limousine and drove along the road, there would be no sense of journey, no sense of giving. Therefore, renunciation is extremely important. We have to renounce our home—our snug, comfortable samsaric world.

There are two types of renunciation: genuine becoming and contentment. The first type of renunciation in Tibetan is *ngejung*: *nge* means "real" or "genuine," and *jung* means "becoming" or "happening"; so *ngejung* is "real becoming." Renunciation is true, real, definite. We are disgusted and put off by the samsaric world we have been living in. The second type of renunciation is a sense of contentment, or *chok-she* in Tibetan. *Chok* means "contentment," "satisfaction," or "enough," and *she* means "knowledge." We know that things are enough as they are. We do not make further demands and we don't insist on having all the local conveniences, but we are satisfied to live in poverty. This does not refer to psychological poverty, however, for practitioners are supposed to have a sense of generosity and richness.

Traditionally there are five paths: the path of accumulation, the path of unification, the path of seeing, the path of meditation, and the path of no more learning.[1]

1. The Path of Accumulation

The path of accumulation is based on getting acquainted with the teachings and the teacher. You are putting in a lot of hard work in order to learn the teachings. It is the layperson's or beginner's level. You are new to the teachings and not yet an accomplished meditator, so you start the whole path right from the beginning—but it is a good way of beginning at the beginning. You do not have to go back to the common path, but this does not mean that you act against common law or that you become a criminal, or anything of that nature. Instead, your attitude is very direct and simple. Although you are a beginner, your approach to the path is not based on the conventional law of goodness and badness. On the path of dharma, behaving well or becoming a good person is not the point. The issue of goodness or wickedness does not particularly belong to the realm of dharma. Dharma has to do with sanity, with issues of clarity and confusion. Dharma is more psychologically oriented than behavior pattern oriented.

The first path, the path of accumulation, is finding your foothold in the teachings as a layperson. Having found that foothold in the teachings, you begin to make the journey upward. In Tibetan, the path of accumulation is *tsog-lam. Tsog* (or *tsok*) means "group," "collection," or "gathering"; *lam* means "path." On the path of accumulation we are working with ourselves and we are inspired to make sacrifices. We accumulate good merit by developing a good attitude and performing good deeds. We cultivate simplicity and sacrifice.

On the path of accumulation we also learn to sacrifice our mind; that is, we don't indulge in our thought process or our subconscious gossip. We give that up by means of the very basic and ordinary discipline of shamatha practice. Usually, whenever we have a bright idea of how to go about something, whenever we have *any* kind of desire, we automatically try to follow it up. We would like to raid the refrigerator, so to speak. We would like apple juice, orange juice, cottage cheese, ice water—anything to avoid boredom. Through shamatha, we discover that we do not need to jump to conclusions or act purely out of impulse. All those impulses are canceled out by the process of mental discipline.

The Mantra of Experience

One of the practices on the path of accumulation is called the "mantra of experience." In this practice, you repeat the four noble truths four different ways, or recite what are called "the sixteen incantations." The reason for reciting the mantra of experience is to increase your sense of identification with the practice and teaching that you have learned. It is to build real conviction, or *ngepar shepa. Ngepar shepa* is not just ordinary conviction, but real conviction, knowing completely and thoroughly. At the level of the path of accumulation, you are proud because for the first time you have heard the four noble truths in their absolute meaning. But although there is intense pride, it is still underdeveloped, so the idea of reciting sixteen incantations is to strengthen your identification with the teachings.

Practicing the mantra of experience cuts the root of being born in the lower realms, and as such, it is very important and profound. In reciting this incantation, you are shifting your conceptualization much closer to the truth. One of the beauties of the hinayana teaching is that you are not looking for a higher goal, but you are simply manipulating your confusion in a wiser way. In that way, you begin to find yourself closer to freedom. You actually begin to see an alternative to samsara.

Reciting the mantra of experience has nothing to do with magic or with calming the mind; it is simply that the more you ponder it, the more you are convinced of its truth. It is a form of brainwashing, but the brain that you wash out is the ego. In reciting the mantra, the whole of existence becomes a manifestation of truth or liberation, and you could identify with it as a totality.

The first set of incantations is: the truth of suffering should be seen; the origin of the suffering should be avoided; the goal should be attained; the path should be actualized.[2]

The second series of incantations is: suffering should be realized as impermanent, the origin of suffering should be realized as impermanent, the goal should be realized as impermanent; the path should be realized as impermanent.

The third set is: suffering should be seen clearly; the origin of suffering should be seen clearly, the goal should be seen clearly, the path should be seen clearly.

The fourth set of incantations is: no suffering, no origin of suffering, no goal, no path.

The first set is familiarizing yourself with the basic logic of the four noble truths. The second set is discovering that the four noble truths do not allow you to develop security, since they are all just transitory experience. With the third set, having seen the transitory nature of that experience, you develop a personal identification with these truths. They should be seen clearly and properly. The fourth set of incantations is that, in actual fact, the only requirement to work on yourself is to cut the suffering, the origin of suffering, the goal, and the path. Therefore, there is no suffering, no origin, no goal, and no path. That is the final statement of vipashyana experience: that we should cut the root of confusion altogether.

Joining Relative and Absolute Truth

When we practice shamatha discipline, we begin to see that our mind is full of stuff. But when we examine our passion, our attachments, and our desires for all sorts of things, we see that they are basically a bad job—purely thought patterns, sand castles, paper tigers. We see that if we wallow in our own lethargy and stupidity, there is no shelter or comfort in that either. By not buying our own habitual thought patterns, we begin to develop discipline and mindfulness.

On the path of accumulation, our experience of mental processes is becoming very real. Passion, aggression, ignorance, and all the subconscious mental activities that take place in our minds become very ordinary and understandable. This leads to a realization of *kündzop*, or relative truth. When we relate with relative truth, we are no longer shocked by our mind. We begin to see the simplicity and the reality of things. When we sit on our cushions and practice, we come across all sorts of thought patterns and desires. Whether we are rereading our autobiography, so to speak, discovering all sorts of choices, thinking we should leave, and or thinking we should stay—all of that is included in the relative truth of our thought patterns.

When we sit and practice, we begin to realize what is known as the transparency and impermanence of time and space. We realize how much we are dwelling on our little things and that we cannot catch any of it and build a house on it. We cannot even lay the foundation. The whole thing keeps shifting under our feet and under our seat. The rug is being pulled out from under us completely, simply from that experience of working with ourselves. Nobody is pulling it, but we find that the rug constantly moves. We begin to feel that we ourselves are moving.

When we realize that we cannot catch hold of phenomena at all, that is what is known as *töndam*, or "absolute truth." There is an absolute quality to the fact that we cannot fool ourselves. We can try to fool our teacher, who tells us to sit; and we might think that we can fool the dharma, which says, "Go sit. That is the only way." But we cannot fool ourselves. We cannot fool our essence. The ground we are sitting on cannot be fooled. That is the two-fold truth of kündzop and töndam. When you put kündzop and töndam together and they become one unit, it becomes possible to make things workable. You are not too much on the side of töndam, or you would become too theoretical; you are not too much on the side of kündzop, or you would become too precise. When you put them together, you begin to realize that there is no problem. The combination of kündzop and töndam works because it is simple and dynamic. You have hot and cold water together, so you can take a really good shower. So kündzop and töndam are both very important; you can't stick with either one separately. Ultimately, through the experience of combining kündzop and töndam on the path of accumulation, you develop a sense of renunciation, simplicity, satisfaction, and contentment in the practice. That is the first of the five paths, the path of accumulation.

2. The Path of Unification

The second path is the path of unification, in which your actions and your psychological state are beginning to work together. When you sit in meditation, you begin to develop a glimpse of sanity, a glimpse of the bodhisattva path. The second path is called the path of unification (*jor-lam* in Tibetan) because we join our mind and body and all our efforts together. It has five categories: faith, exertion, recollection, one-pointedness, and intellect.

Faith

The first category is *tepa*, which means "faith." We feel very steady and confident in what we have done so far. We appreciate what we have done. We realize what should be avoided and what should be cultivated. That is, subconscious gossip and grasping should be avoided; steadiness of mind should be cultivated.

Tepa also involves delightfulness. We realize that we are not in the dark as far as our practice is concerned. We know our directions, roughly speaking, where we are and where we are going.

Exertion

The second category is *tsöndrü*, or "exertion." When we have realized what we are doing, we develop confidence. We realize the isness or the suchness of the truth that we have been told. We experience a sense of upliftedness as a result of shamatha discipline, and from that we develop further exertion. If we are served a dish that we like, and if we like the cook and the restaurant, we don't mind eating that dish a second, third, or fourth time because we know that it is going to be good. There is a sense of delight in going back again and again to the same restaurant. Similarly, exertion does not mean taking pains; it means appreciation. Appreciation makes things more and more enjoyable; and when we enjoy something, we do it over and over, even though there is tremendous effort involved. On the path of unification, our shamatha practice is becoming enjoyable, so we do it again and again, eternally.

Recollection

The third category of the path of unification is *trenpa*, which literally means "recollection." Recollection means that what you have done and what you have experienced are not forgotten, but remain as part of your awareness and mindfulness. There is a sense of respect and genuine appreciation for what you have received and what you are doing. Recollection means experiencing what you have done, which is your practice; and what you are, which is your state of mind. Recollection is very awake and precise. If somebody tells you that you have a chore in the kitchen at five o'clock, it is very simple: you just do it. There are no hang-ups involved.

Memory, in contrast, could be based on nostalgia for samsara. For instance, you might have had a bad fight, and by remembering it, in some perverted way you are able to maintain your whole being. You also might indulge in nostalgia for goodness, as a sort of psychological orgy. Such memories begin to have no gap, so you have no chance to be precise and clear.

One-Pointedness

The fourth category, *tingdzin*, meaning "meditation" or "samadhi," in this case refers to one-pointedness. You never lose track of anything; you develop tremendous awareness. Your mind becomes very focused, very accurate. You appreciate sense perceptions, but you are not trapped by them, and they do not create samsaric, karmic problems. Because you are able to perceive, to appreciate, and to focus your mind one-pointedly, you develop a sense of composure.

Intellect

The fifth category is *sherap*, or prajna in Sanskrit, which in this context means "intellect." You understand how to see things, how to separate various experiences. There might still be occasional upheavals—both experiences of satisfaction or achievement, and experiences of obstacles and doubts—but you can clearly separate what should be avoided from what should be cultivated. There is both clarity and discrimination.

Through those five categories of the path of unification, we are able to hold things together, as though we were holding the fort. We do not experience any chaos; instead, we begin to feel that everything hangs together. That is why this path is known as the path of unification.

3. The Path of Seeing

In this path you develop further clarity in distinguishing or discriminating the different approaches to reality according to the buddhadharma. The path of seeing is *thong-lam* in Tibetan. *Thong* means "seeing," and *lam*, again, is "path." The path of seeing is at a much more advanced level than the path of unification. You begin to see how the path operates and how it could be applicable to yourself.

The Seven Limbs of Enlightenment

There are seven categories in the path of seeing, known as the seven limbs of enlightenment, or *bodhi:* recollection, separating dharmas, exertion, joy, being thoroughly trained, samadhi, and equilibrium. In Tibetan this is called *changchup yenlak dün.* *Changchup* is "enlightenment," *yenlak* is "limb," and *dün* is "seven."

RECOLLECTION. The first of the seven limbs is *trenpa,* or recollection (which came up previously as the third category of the path of unification). Recollection means not forgetting the path of seeing, the sense of forward vision. You do not stay in one place, trying to be a faithful old person. Instead, you develop further ambition, not in the negative sense but in the sense of going forward. That ambition is triggered by memory, or recollection.

SEPARATING DHARMAS. The second limb is connected with *sherap,* or intellect. As in the previous path, there is a sense of discrimination, of separating dharmas and realizing the isness of things. There is no uncertainty about experience. In each of the paths you need sherap, which is connected with actually being able to open up. On the path of unification, prajna was partial, somewhat embryonic, but on the path of seeing it is closer to complete prajna. However, it is still nothing like the perfect knowledge of the *paramita* level, which is much superior.[3]

EXERTION. The third limb is *tsöndrü,* exertion, which in this case has a slightly different meaning than previously. In cultivating a constant furthering of vision on the path of seeing, you never give up, you never settle down to the situation at hand. You have the positive ambition of forward vision.

JOY. The fourth limb is *gawa,* which means "joy." You are able to take care of both body and mind. This is not a situation where your mind is highly developed but your body is rotting, or your body is well cared for but your mind is rotting. Instead, your body and mind are synchronized, well connected. The samsaric hassles of dealing with your mind and body begin to subside. You are able to handle your body and mind completely, so you develop a sense of health. You know how to avoid unnecessary hassles: you don't collect further garbage in the interest of either mind or body. The joy of simplicity begins to develop, along with a sense of precision, genuineness, and obviousness.

BEING THOROUGHLY TRAINED. The fifth limb, *shinjang*, means being thoroughly soothed or trained. Your body and mind are totally relaxed. As a result of shamatha practice, your mind and body are tamed, trained, developed. There is a tremendous sense of humor and relaxation, and a sense of openness, gentleness, and goodness. You are beginning to feel the effect of your practice. It is beginning to work, and you feel positive. It is like coming out of a steam bath: your muscles have relaxed; you feel so healthy.

SAMADHI. The sixth limb is *tingdzin*, which means "samadhi" or "one-pointedness." You are focused, one-pointed, and at the same time, you are humble. In spite of your achievements, you never get puffed up.

EQUILIBRIUM. The seventh and final limb is *tang-nyom*, which means "equilibrium." You are not subject to sluggishness or laziness, and you are also free from wandering and excitable mind. A sense of evenness is taking place all the time. You are neither disturbed nor completely asleep. It should be quite clear that equilibrium does not mean becoming a jellyfish or an even-tempered ape. In this case, you have command of the whole world. You have tremendous confidence in dealing with your world; therefore, you don't have to push anything either positively or negatively. You don't have to dwell on anything or exaggerate anything.

That concludes the seven limbs of bodhi, the seven categories of the path of seeing.

4. The Path of Meditation

The fourth path is called the path of meditation, or *gom-lam*. Traditionally, *gom* means "to think about"; in Buddhist terms, it means "to meditate." In the nontheistic tradition, meditation means just meditation, rather than meditation *on* anything, and *lam*, again, means "path." On the path of meditation, your sense of style begins to be closer to an enlightened style rather than a neurotic style.

On the path of meditation, you begin to cut karma. Karma is based on fundamental ignorance. Whenever there are two, you and other, that is already the beginning of a karmic situation. When you not only have you and other, but you begin to elaborate on that, you are at the level of the second nidana, or *samskara* (formation). You have begun to roll the wheel of karma.

Fundamental ignorance is pre-dual. In the phrase "I am," pre-dual ignorance is pre-"am"—it is the "I" stage. Duality does not yet exist, so calling it nondual would be jumping the gun. Although there is no duality, however, there is still a false sense of suchness or isness. There is a kind of anti-shunyata sense of existence or fullness, which has to be cut.

Although fundamental ignorance begins to be cut on the path of meditation, it is not thoroughly cut at this point. You have cut the consequences of karma, but not the causes. When you cut both the consequences and the causes—the karmic situation altogether—that is the path of no more learning, which is enlightenment.

The Noble Eightfold Path

There are eight categories of the path of meditation, which are collectively known as the noble eightfold path.[4] The eight limbs of the noble path are perfect view, perfect understanding, perfect speech, perfect end of karma, perfect livelihood, perfect effort, perfect recollection, and perfect meditation. At the level of the path of seeing, you began to see, and now you are able to make something of it. Your whole being has been thoroughly trained physically, psychologically, and in terms of working with others.

PERFECT VIEW. The first limb of the noble path is *yangdak tawa*. *Yangdak* means "perfect" and *tawa* is "view." So *yangdak tawa* means "perfect view." We add *yangdak*, or *perfect*, before all eight limbs. Perfect view means that you are able to cut through the absorptions and fixed views of your previous experiences, which may have made you somewhat sleepy and theoretical. At the level of the path of seeing, you might have been able to gaze at the ultimate truth, but tawa enables you actually to see through. "View" does not mean good view or bad view, but simply understanding things as they are. You are able to cut through and you are able to analyze and to theorize in the positive sense. This does not mean that you are scholastic or that you psychologize, but you are able to see the differences between the first, second, and third paths. You are able to see how things work geographically and chronologically. Because you can see through things at this point, you are becoming less dependent on your teacher, or elder. Your elder is wise and scholarly, brilliant and compassionate, but you don't have to depend on him or her. You are able to see through by yourself; therefore, you are becoming somewhat independent.

PERFECT UNDERSTANDING. The second limb is *yangdak tokpa*, "perfect understanding," or "perfect realization." You have learned how to relax. Based on what you have experienced, there is no questioning and no doubt. You have understood, and you appreciate what you have understood; therefore, you learn how to relax and let yourself go.

PERFECT SPEECH. The third limb is *yangdak ngak*, "perfect speech." You have found a way of declaring yourself fully and thoroughly—how you are, why you are, what you are—without being arrogant, aggressive, or too humble. You have learned how to be moderate in presenting yourself. *Ngak*, "speech," does not refer simply to how you speak, but also to how you reflect yourself to the world—your general demeanor or decorum. You can become reasonable, decent, and enlightened.

PERFECT END OF KARMA. The fourth limb is *yangdak le kyi tha*, which literally means the perfect "end of karma." *Tha* means "end," *kyi* is "of," *le* means "karma." You begin to understand how to prevent karmic cause and results suddenly, precisely, and thoroughly. The end of karma means that you might return once or twice to the world because your immediate karmic situation has not yet been cut through; however, your previous karma has been cut through already by means of perfect view, perfect understanding, and perfect speech. Your habitual patterns and your whole behavior begin to be more accurate, more enlightened. By behaving naturally, you are able to cut through karma and karmic consequences.

In cutting through karma, you are constantly dealing with ignorance, the first nidana. Since volitional action is driven by ignorance, if you are able to cut through that ignorance, you stop the course of volitional action. You can do so because at the level of the path of meditation, your style of relating with the dharma becomes very natural and instinctive. In contrast, the style of volitional action is that you are always looking forward to the next carrot. You see the carrot as somewhat distant from you, and you work yourself up to run from here to there, from yourself to the carrot. In doing so, you crank up more karma; and when you get there, you end up with the next karmic cause. So you end up with a lot more karma—and you have created the carrot, as well! We never say that in the samsaric world, but in the enlightened world we can say it.

In cutting karma, disgust and renunciation are regarded as important. Although it is a neat, ugly trick for you to put the carrot in front of yourself, you know you shouldn't be doing that. By renouncing that, you are able to cut the second nidana, which is samskara, or impulsive accumulation. At this point, you are becoming so accomplished in that, that even if you plant a karmic promise in other people, you are able to cut through their karmic cause and effect as well.

PERFECT LIVELIHOOD. Number five is *yangdak tsowa*, which means perfect livelihood. Because you are able to handle karmic cause and effect, you can also relate with your own life and livelihood. You do not have to depend on others. You have enough skill to be able to handle your livelihood thoroughly and fully.

PERFECT EFFORT. The sixth limb is *yangdak tsölwa,* which means perfect effort. This has the sense of not holding back but exerting yourself. You have tremendous energy. You cultivate genuine energy, in both working with yourself and working with others. As you go from path to path, you develop more and more effort, more and more industry. You begin to become a decent person, no longer a nuisance.

PERFECT RECOLLECTION. The seventh limb is *yangdak trenpa,* "perfect recollection." As before, trenpa refers to a sense of mindfulness, or one-pointed mind, and to the recollection of your previous experiences.

PERFECT MEDITATION. The eighth and last limb of the noble path is *yangdak tingdzin,* or "perfect meditation." In this context, tingdzin means that you are able to enter into certain samadhis. You begin to look ahead toward the notion of enlightenment. At this point, you might be able to completely cut through twofold ego (ego of self and ego of dharmas).[5]

5. The Path of No More Learning

The final path is the path of no more learning, which is the attainment of enlightenment. In Tibetan it is *mi-lop-lam.* Since at the hinayana level, you have only a very rough idea about how enlightenment takes place, the fifth path includes the remainder of the mahayana path and the attainment of enlightenment.

Progress on the Path

The five paths, which are very complicated and complex, have been briefly described to give you an idea of a student's psychological development through the practice of meditation. In that way, you can have guidelines on the path, not only from your teacher or your friends or neighbors, but from yourself. There is a journey taking place, and if you ask who the judge is, I think that you yourself are the best judge of the level of pain and confusion you are experiencing.

When we discuss the path, or Buddhism in general, we have to face the fact that there is something corny taking place. We say that we are not striving for the result of enlightenment, that we are not interested in that, that we don't have an ego, so we are free of all that. But at the same time we *do* talk about enlightenment. We say we are going to attain enlightenment, that we are going to become better persons. We have to face that obvious fact. There is no point trying to make ourselves more sophisticated than everybody else on earth who has followed a spiritual path. It may be disturbing to realize that you have fallen back into the common logic, to realize that everybody is searching for pleasure and so are you. However, that is the fact. In Buddhism, we talk about decreasing neurosis, which automatically means decreasing ego-oriented pain. We talk about attaining enlightenment—a state in which there is no need for security, but ultimate security develops. Without such logic, the Buddha could not truly teach human beings at all.

The teaching exists in order for you to get better, in order for you to develop; that's a known fact. You could say that you're not interested in any such thing, thinking that's the best thing to say, but if you're not interested in anything like that, you've caught yourself already. You think you're very smart, but you are fooling yourself. You have to become stupid, dumb, and simple-minded, in a sense, in order to commit yourself to the teachings and the path. And whether you like it or not, Buddhism is a doctrine of some kind. Even though it may be a transcendental doctrine, it is still a doctrine. So let us not try to be too sophisticated. There is no such thing as "cool dharma" or "hip truth." If it's the truth, it's the truth.

On the Buddhist path you are expected to develop certain states of mind, you are expected to show certain signs. You are also expected to share these things with the rest of your brothers and sisters on earth and to work with them as well. But none of this is regarded as a good thing to do—it's just ordinary flow, like a river. If a river flowed backward or a waterfall went upstream, we would think either that we were hallucinating or that something was wrong with the landscape. Similarly, the logic of the path has to flow, just like water is always expected to flow down and slowly make its journey to the ocean. Such norms are obvious. The sun is expected to rise in the east and set in the west—we can't be very hip and unconventional; we can't change the direction of the sun.

In terms of signs on the path, you are not particularly waiting for something to happen, but when it happens, it happens—and it is sure to happen sooner or later. However, there is not the expectation that once you get to the next level, you are going to be okay. In fact, it is quite possible that at each new level you discover more problems. For instance, attaining arhatship sounds good, but once you get there, you might find more problems and troubles. As you progress along the path, you are in a constant process of becoming more and more intelligent. The more intelligent you become and the more aware you are of all the details of the overall vision, the more things you find wrong with yourself.

You don't particularly expect happiness out of the path. However, you do expect sophistication and a sense of relief or confidence that something is actually happening. You don't have to know where you are on the path, but you need to know that you are moving and that you are going to get to your destination. However, if you are too concerned with getting from here to there as fast as possible, you find yourself in a lot of pain. It is not how fast you can get there but the movement that matters. On the path, you are not stuck, but you are constantly moving. As soon as you switch on the stove, the food is cooking.

The whole path may seem to be at the folk level, but the teachings are not particularly folksy—nor, for that matter, are they for scholars, magicians, royalty, or monks and nuns. The teachings are not *designed* for anything. The dharma is straightforward teaching. It contains certain common basic truths; otherwise, you could not communicate it and you could not appreciate it. No matter how many restaurants you might eat in or how fancy they may be, you still eat by putting food in your mouth; there's no other way to eat. No restaurant offers food to consume in any other way.

In working with the five paths, you begin with the first path and the practice of shamatha. As you go on, you begin to evolve, and there is some sort of progress report. The five paths might seem hard to relate to, but they are real and you could aspire to them. There is nothing unreasonable about them: they are both reasonable and possible. If you aspire to joy, you can attain it, because you have joy in you. Similarly, you also have exertion, concentration, and prajna. Those things are all household terms, nothing exotic or primitive. So the message is very simple: it is possible and you can do it. You can work with the four noble truths.

Because suffering is fundamental, there is a fundamental cure for it as well. That cure is *saddharma*: real (*sat*) dharma. Real dharma can actually cure fundamental pain; that is why it is known as *sat*, or "truth." It is genuine dharma. Fundamental suffering is based on a basic karmic mishap, arising from ignorance. However, when you begin to work with your state of mind, you realize the consequences of your ignorance and you see how you can correct it. Your fundamental ignorance is the cause of all karmic coincidence, but instead of stupidly going along with that, you begin to wake up by means of meditation practice. You are aware of trying to cut through twofold ego fixation—the ego of dharmas and the ego of self—and you are beginning to knock the guts out of the whole thing. You are putting lots of effort and energy into that. It is very straightforward.

Practice is fundamental. It is a genuine cure. You have a genuine ego and genuine suffering, with cures to match. It has been said that dharma is medicine, the teacher is a physician, and you are the patient. If you have a sickness that medicine can cure, the teacher can diagnose you and treat it. And as you go on through the yanas, from the hinayana to the vajrayana, that cure becomes much tougher and more accurate. That is the notion of saddharma. Saddharma is the ultimate cure because it deals not only with the symptoms, but with the sickness itself.

THE PRACTICE OF MEDITATION

Basic Instructions & Guidelines

CHÖGYAM TRUNGPA

T HE PRACTICE OF MEDITATION is not so much about a hypo-
thetical attainment of enlightenment as about leading a
good life. In order to learn how to lead a good life, a spotless life,
we need continual awareness that relates with life constantly,
directly, and very simply.

The attitude that brings about mindfulness and awareness is
not an opinionated one. Mindfulness is simply about a sense of
being; you are in contact, you are actually being there. When you
sit on the meditation cushion, you feel you are sitting there and
that you actually exist. You don't need to encourage or sustain
your sense of being.

We might actually question what is the purpose of meditation,
what happens next, but actually the idea of meditation is to
develop an entirely different way of dealing with things, where
you have no purpose at all. One is not constantly on the way to
somewhere, or rather one is on the way and at the destination at
the same time.

Our posture in sitting practice is important. Sitting cross-
legged is recommended, with the spine straight, not stiff, so that
the breath is not strained or inhibited. However, imposing too
much intensity on the body will undermine the whole thing,
so you can rearrange your posture as necessary. If there is some
physical problem that makes sitting on the floor too difficult, a
chair can be used, but it is best not to lean against the back.

Eyes remain open, but if we are paying too much attention to visual details and colors, the head and neck may tighten. We simply rest the gaze slightly downward without trying to focus on anything.

As you exhale, follow the breath outward. Try to actually identify with it rather than just watching it. The in-breath naturally follows when the lungs are empty, just let it happen without particularly paying attention to it.

It is very important to avoid becoming overly solemn or feeling that one is taking part in some special ritual. One should simply try to identify oneself with the breath; there are no ideas or analyzing involved.

Whenever thoughts arise, just observe them as thoughts and label them "thinking." What usually happens when we have thoughts is that we absorb ourselves and cease to be aware that we are thinking at all. One should try not to suppress thoughts in meditation, but just try to see their transitory nature, their translucent nature. We do not become involved in them or reject them, but simply acknowledge them and then come back to the awareness of breathing. There should be no deliberate effort to control and no attempt to be peaceful. Our thoughts simply cease to be the VIPs in our lives.

On the other hand, there is no implication that by sitting and meditating, coming back to the breath, we have found a way to avoid problems, an escape from one point to another. Meditation is not a quick cure or cover-up for the complicated or embarrassing aspects of ourselves. It is a way of life. It is extremely important to persist in our practice without second-guessing ourselves through disappointments, elations, or whatever. We might actually begin to see the world we carry with us in a more open, refreshing way. Meditation is very much a matter of exercise, a working practice. It is not a matter of going into some imaginary depth, but of widening and expanding outward.

These instructions are presented as the basic foundation of meditation practice. It is important to follow these guidelines to ensure a good understanding at the beginning.

OUTLINE OF TEACHINGS

The numbered lists of teachings in this book have been organized into outline style here as a study aid. The lists are in order of appearance in the text.

The First Noble Truth: Suffering

I. The Eight Types of Suffering
- A. Inherited Suffering
  1. Birth
  2. Old age
  3. Sickness
  4. Death

- B. Suffering of the Period between Birth and Death
  5. Coming across what is not desirable
  6. Not being able to hold on to what is desirable
  7. Not getting what you want

- C. General Misery
  8. General misery

II. The Three Patterns of Suffering
- A. The Suffering of Suffering
  1. Birth
  2. Old age
  3. Sickness

       4. Death

       5. Coming across what is not desirable

  B. The Suffering of Change

       6. Trying to hold on to what is desirable

       7. Not getting, or not knowing, what you want

  C. All-pervasive Suffering

       8. General misery

The Second Noble Truth: The Origin of Suffering

  I. The Seven Ego-Oriented Patterns

    A. Regarding the five skandhas as belonging to oneself

    B. Protecting oneself from impermanence

    C. Belief that one's view is best

    D. Believing in the extreme of nihilism or eternalism

    E. Passion

    F. Aggression

    G. Ignorance

  II. The Six Root Kleshas (Conflicting Emotions)

    A. Desire

    B. Anger

    C. Pride

    D. Ignorance

    E. Doubt

    F. Opinion

  III. The Karmic Patterns That Lead to Suffering

    A. Unmeritorious karma

      1. Body

        a. Taking life

        b. Stealing

        c. Sexual misconduct

    2. Speech

        d. Telling lies

        e. Intrigue

        f. Negative words

        g. Gossip

    3. Mind

        h. Envy

        i. Hoping to create harm

        j. Disbelieving in sacredness

B. Meritorious karma

    1. Respect for life

    2. Generosity

    3. Sexual wholesomeness

    4. Truthfulness

    5. Straightforwardness

    6. Good wisdom

    7. Simplicity

    8. Openness

    9. Gentleness

    10. Sacredness

C. The six types of karmic consequence

    1. The power of volitional action

        a. Good beginning, bad ending

        b. Bad beginning, good ending

        c. Bad beginning, bad ending

        d. Good beginning, good ending

    2. Experiencing what you have planted

        a. Immediately

        b. Later

    c. Ripening from a previous birth

  3. White karmic consequences

    a. Emulating the three jewels

    b. Emulating and appreciating somebody else's virtue

    c. Practicing the dharma

  4. Changing the karmic flow by forceful action

  5. Shared karmic situations

    a. National karma

    b. Individual karma within national karma

  6. Interaction of intention and action

    a. White intention, white action

    b. Black intention, black action

    c. White intention, black action

    d. Black intention, white action

The Third Noble Truth: The Cessation of Suffering

I. The Three Categories of Samsara

  A. The seed of samsara: bewilderment

  B. The cause of samsara: fixation

  C. The effect of samsara: suffering

II. The Four Ways of Developing Wholesomeness

  A. Relating properly to food

  B. Relating properly to sleep and rest

  C. Meticulousness

  D. Meditation

III. The Twelve Aspects of Cessation

  A. Nature

    1. Origin: meditative absorption

      2. What should be given up: neurosis

      3. Path to be cultivated: simplicity

  B. Profundity

  C. Sign

  D. Ultimate

  E. Incompletion

  F. Signs of completion

  G. Without ornament

  H. Adorned

  I. With omission

  J. Without omission

  K. Especially supreme

  L. Beyond calculation

      1. Renunciation

      2. Complete purification

      3. Worn out

      4. Passionlessness

      5. Cessation

      6. Complete peace

      7. Subsiding

The Fourth Noble Truth: The Path

  I. The Sequence of the Path

    A. Overcoming the notion of eternity

    B. Overcoming the search for pleasure

    C. Realizing the possibility of emptiness

    D. Encountering egolessness

  II. The Four Qualities of the Path

    A. Path: searching for the real meaning of suchness

B. Insight: through clarity, transcending neurosis

C. Practice: associating with basic sanity

D. Fruition: permanent nirvana

III. The Five Paths

A. The Path of Accumulation (*tsog-lam*)

1. The mantra of experience: the sixteen incantations
   a. First set of incantations
      1. Suffering should be seen
      2. The origin of the suffering should be avoided
      3. The goal should be attained
      4. The path should be actualized
   b. Second set of incantations
      5. Suffering should be realized as impermanent
      6. The origin of suffering should be realized as impermanent
      7. The goal should be realized as impermanent
      8. The path should be realized as impermanent
   c. Third set of incantations
      9. Suffering should be seen clearly
      10. The origin of suffering should be seen clearly
      11. The goal should be seen clearly
      12. The path should be seen clearly
   d. Fourth set of incantations
      13. No suffering
      14. No origin of suffering
      15. No goal
      16. No path
2. Twofold truth
   a. Relative truth (*kündzop*)
   b. Absolute truth (*töndam*)

B. The Path of Unification (*jor-lam*)

   1. The five categories

      a. Faith

      b. Exertion

      c. Recollection

      d. One-pointedness

      e. Intellect

C. The Path of Seeing (*thong-lam*)

   1. The seven limbs of enlightenment

      a. Recollection

      b. Separating dharmas

      c. Exertion

      d. Joy

      e. Being thoroughly trained

      f. Samadhi

      g. Equilibrium

D. The Path of Meditation (*gom-lam*)

   1. The noble eightfold path

      a. Perfect view

      b. Perfect understanding

      c. Perfect speech

      d. Perfect end of karma

      e. Perfect livelihood

      f. Perfect effort

      g. Perfect recollection

      h. Perfect meditation

E. The Path of No More Learning (*mi-lop-lam*)

NOTES

Chapter 1

1. Trungpa Rinpoche employed the psychological term *neurosis*, not in the strictly Freudian sense, but to refer to the common human experience of conflicting emotions. He preferred to present the spiritual path as a journey from neurosis to sanity, rather than using more religious or philosophical terminology.

2. In the Buddhist system of six realms, the three higher realms are the god realm, the jealous-god realm, and the human realm; the three lower realms are the animal realm, the hungry ghost realm, and the hell realm. These realms can refer to psychological states or to aspects of Buddhist cosmology. For further commentary, see Chögyam Trungpa, *The Myth of Freedom* (Boston: Shambhala Publications, 1988).

Chapter 2

1. The traditional Buddhist understanding of this form of suffering is not getting what you want; Trungpa Rinpoche expands it to include not knowing what you want.

Chapter 5

1. According to *Mind in Buddhist Psychology*, translated by Herbert Guenther and Leslie Kawamura (Emeryville, Calif.: Dharma Publishing, 1975), the twenty secondary kleshas are indignation, resentment, slyness-concealment, spite, jealousy, avarice, deceit, dishonesty, mental inflation, malice, shamelessness, lack of sense of propriety, gloominess, ebullience, lack of trust, laziness, unconcern, forgetfulness, inattentiveness, and desultoriness.

2. In different contexts, Trungpa Rinpoche uses variant forms of the primary six kleshas, most commonly (1) passion, aggression, ignorance,

arrogance/pride, envy/jealousy, and greed/stinginess/meanness/
holding back, and (2) desire, anger, pride, ignorance, doubt, and
opinion.

3. The word *karma* has many meanings. Most simply it means action
   and is related to the idea of cause and effect, in the sense that past
   actions have shaped our present situation, and present actions shape
   our future circumstances. Although we cannot change the circumstances we are born into, it is possible to affect our future by the
   choices and actions we perform in the present. Teachings on karma
   are closely linked with the notion of rebirth—the view that in this
   life, and over many lifetimes, our experience is not one solid thing,
   but a recurrent arising, manifesting, and dissolving.

4. In discussing karma, Trungpa Rinpoche places the teaching of transforming bad karmic circumstances into good ones in the context of
   the possibility of transcending karmic cause and effect altogether.

Chapter 8

1. The five paths—the path of accumulation, the path of unification,
   the path of seeing, the path of meditation, and the path of no
   more learning—can be used to describe any of the three yanas.
   Trungpa Rinpoche is drawing a distinction between a hinayana
   understanding of the path of no more learning and the vajrayana
   understanding of that path.

2. In general, Trungpa Rinpoche preferred to use Sanskrit terminology,
   such as *dhyanas* for meditative absorptions. However, at times he
   also used the Pali term *jhanas* (Pali being the language of hinayana
   texts) in referring to the meditative absorptions.

3. The great logician Nagarjuna (ca. second to third centuries) developed a dialectical approach of systematically undercutting any
   attempt to establish a solid logical position. This became the basis of
   the "Middle Way," or madhyamaka, school.

4. Trungpa Rinpoche trained in both the Kagyü and Nyingma schools
   of Tibetan Buddhism.

5. Trungpa Rinpoche uses *brahma* to refer to a more personalized
   notion of brahmahood in the sense of Godhead (as in the Hindu
   trinity of Brahma the Creator, Vishnu the Preserver, and Shiva the

Destroyer); and *brahman* (the Hindu term for the Absolute) to refer to a more sophisticated level of understanding.

Chapter 10

1. This division of the path into five distinct stages is attributed to Atisha Dipankara (990–1055) in his work *Lamp on the Way to Enlightenment* (Skt.: *Bodhipathapradipa*). It is also discussed in *The Jewel Ornament of Liberation* by Gampopa.

2. The first four incantations are used as the epigraphs at the beginning of each of the four divisions of this book.

3. In the *1973 Hinayana-Mahayana Seminary Transcripts,* in reference to prajna and the five paths, Trungpa Rinpoche places the complete expression of prajnaparamita on the fourth path, the path of meditation, which includes levels 2–10 of the traditional stages, or *bhumis,* of the bodhisattva path. An ordinary student begins with the path of accumulation; catches a glimpse of mahayana possibilities at the path of unification; enters the first bhumi at the path of seeing; practices bhumis 2–10 at the path of meditation; and attains complete enlightenment on the path of no more learning.

4. Trungpa Rinpoche also discusses the eightfold path in *The Myth of Freedom and the Way of Meditation.*

5. The belief in an "I" and the belief in an "other" are both cut through. Neither the self nor external phenomena are seen to be inherently and independently existing.

GLOSSARY

This glossary includes terms in English, Tibetan (Tib.), Sanskrit (Skt.), Pali, and Japanese (Jpn.). Tibetan terms are spelled phonetically followed by the transliteration in parentheses.

abhidharma (Skt.). Supreme dharma. The Buddhist teachings can be divided into three parts, called "the three baskets," or *tripitika:* the sutras (teachings of the Buddha), the vinaya (teachings on conduct), and the abhidharma (teachings on philosophy and psychology). According to Trungpa, abhidharma can be thought of as the "patterns of the dharma."

aggregate. *See* skandha.

arhat (Skt.). Worthy one. In Tibetan, *drachompa* (dgra bcom pa), "one who has conquered the enemy" of conflicting emotions and grasping at a self-entity. A fully accomplished practitioner of the hinayana path who has achieved liberation from the sufferings of samsara.

avidya (Skt.). (Tib.: marikpa; ma rig pa). Fundamental ignorance, the first nidana. For the klesha of ignorance, *see* timuk.

basic goodness. A term used in the Shambhala teachings of Chögyam Trungpa Rinpoche to describe the primordial state of purity, or the wholesomeness innate in all sentient beings. Said to be like a reservoir, it can be tapped to rouse wisdom and compassion. For more on basic goodness and the Shambhala tradition, see *Shambhala: The Sacred Path of the Warrior.*

bodhi (Skt.). Awake. (Tib.: changchup; byang chub). Enlightenment.

bodhisattva (Skt.). Awake being. In Tibetan, *changchup sempa* (byang chub sems dpa'), "hero of the enlightened mind." A person who has completely overcome confusion and who is committed to cultivating compassion and wisdom through the practice of the six paramitas (transcendent actions) in order to free all beings from suffering.

buddha/Buddha (Skt.). (Tib.: sang-gye; sangs rgyas). Awakened one. In a general sense, *buddha* (lowercase b) may refer to the principle of enlightenment or to any enlightened being. In particular, *the Buddha* (uppercase B) refers to the historical Buddha, Shakyamuni.

buddha in the palm of your hand. An expression in Buddhism used to describe the already-perfect condition of basic wakefulness that every human being intrinsically possesses.

buddha nature. *See* tathagatagarbha.

buddhadharma (Skt.). The teachings of the Buddha.

chakravartin (Skt.). One who turns the wheel. A universal monarch; in ancient Vedic and Buddhist literature, a king who rules the entire world by his wisdom and virtue. The idea of a universal monarch and the establishment of enlightened society plays a significant role in Chögyam Trungpa's presentation of Buddhist and Shambhala teachings.

changchup yenlak dün (Tib.: btang chub yan lag bdun). The seven limbs of enlightenment.

chok-she (Tib.: chog shes). Sense of contentment; literally, "contentment/knowledge." One of the two types of renunciation.

devaloka (Skt.). The god realm, one of six realms of existence into which beings are born. *See* note 2 for Chapter 1 on page 127.

dharma (Skt.). Truth, or law. Specifically, the buddhadharma, the higher dharma, or teachings of the Buddha. Higher dharma is the subtle understanding of the world: how mind works, how samsara perpetuates itself, how it is transcended, and so on. Lower dharma is how things work on the mundane level, for example, how water boils.

dharmas (Skt.). Phenomena, objects of perception.

dhyana (Skt.). (Pali: jhana). Meditation or meditative absorption.

drippa (Tib.: sgrib pa). Defilements, obscurations, and blockages—cognitive or emotional fog.

dug-ngal (Tib.: sdug bsngal). Suffering, anxiety, dissatisfaction. *See* duhkha.

duhkha (Skt.) (Tib.: dug-ngal; sdug bsngal). Suffering. The first of the four noble truths. Physical and psychological suffering of all kinds, including the subtle but all-pervading frustration experienced with regard to the impermanence and insubstantiality of all things.

dzinpa (Tib.: 'dzin pa). Holding on, fixation.

ego. A seemingly solid self that is in fact both transitory and changeable and therefore prone to suffering. A personality imputed from the five aggregates (skandhas). *See* twofold ego.

ego of dharmas. *See* two-fold ego.

ego of self. *See* two-fold ego.

eightfold path, noble In the context of this volume, eight aspects of the path of meditation: (1) perfect view: yangdak tawa (Tib.: yang dag lta ba); (2) perfect understanding: yangdak tokpa (yang dag rtog pa); (3) perfect speech: yangdak ngak (yang dag ngag); (4) perfect end of karma: yangdak le kyi tha (yang dag las kyi mtha'); (5) perfect livelihood: yangdak tsowa (yang dag 'tsho ba); (6) perfect effort: yangdak tsölwa (yang dag rtsol wa); (7) perfect recollection: yangdak trenpa (yang dag dran pa); (8) perfect meditation: yangdak tingdzin (yang dag ting 'dzin).

eternalism/nihilism. Extreme beliefs that perpetuate ego fixation. The view that things are solid and everlasting (eternalism) as one extreme and the view that things are empty and meaningless (nihilism) as the other.

gawa (Tib.: dga' ba). Joy. One of the seven limbs of enlightenment.

gokpa (Tib.: 'gog pa; Skt.: nirodha). Cessation. *See* nirodha.

gomden (Tib.: sgom gdan). A rectangular block-shaped meditation cushion.

gom-lam (Tib.: sgom lam). Path of meditation. *See* paths, five.

Great Eastern Sun. An important image in the Shambhala tradition, representing indestructible wakefulness. Being spontaneously present, it radiates peace and confidence. Being brilliant, it illuminates the way of discipline. Since it shines over all, heaven, earth, and humans find their proper place. It manifests as living one's life with forward vision, gentleness, and fearlessness.

hinayana (Skt.). Narrow or lesser vehicle. In the three-yana path of Tibetan Buddhism—hinayana, mahayana, and vajrayana—the hinayana establishes the foundation. It provides the essential instruction that serves as a basis for the other two vehicles (yanas).

jhana (Pali). Meditative absorption. The jhanas are progressive stages of meditative absorption. According to Trungpa Rinpoche, attachment to such absorption states is an obstacle leading one to become trapped in the god realm. Such experiences are a distraction from the path of awakening and should be avoided.

jor-lam (Tib.: sbyor lam). Path of unification. *See* paths, five.

karma (Skt.). Action. The chain reaction process of action and result. According to the doctrine of cause and effect, our present experience is a product of previous actions and volitions, and future conditions depend on what we do in the present. *See* note 3 for Chapter 5 on page 128.

karmic seeds. All actions, whether of thought, word, or deed, are like seeds that will eventually bear fruit in terms of experience, whether in this or a future lifetimes. *See* karma.

kaya(s), three (Skt.). The three bodies of a buddha: the nirmanakaya (body), sambhogakaya, (speech), and dharmakaya (mind). *Nirmanakaya* (Tib.: *tülku;* sprul sku) means "emanation body," "form body," or "body of manifestation." It is the communication of awakened mind through form—specifically, through embodiment as a human being. *Sambhogakaya* (Tib.: *longku;* longs sku), "enjoyment body," is the energetic environment of compassion and communication linking the dharmakaya and the nirmanakaya. The *dharmakaya* (Tib.: *chöku;* chos sku), or "the body of dharma" is the aspect of realization beyond form or limit, time or space.

khorwa (Tib.: 'khor ba; Skt.: samsara). To spin. Cyclic existence; the vicious cycle of transmigratory existence. *See* samsara.

kleshas (Skt.). (Tib.: nyönmong). Conflicting emotion or defilements. Trungpa Rinpoche referred to kleshas as "neuroses" and to enlightenment as "sanity." Kleshas are properties that dull the mind and are the basis for all unwholesome actions. The three main kleshas are passion, aggression, and ignorance. There are also enumerations of six root kleshas and twenty subsidiary kleshas. *See* nyönmong künjung; nyönmong kyi drippa.

kündzop (Tib.: kun rdzob). Relative or conventional truth.

künjung (Tib.: kun 'byung; Skt.: samudaya). Origin, the origin of suffering. The origin of suffering can be traced to fundamental ignorance and to desire. It is fueled by conflicting emotions (kleshas) and harmful actions (karma). The *künjung of karma* brings about external suffering by acting upon others as a result of the arising of the kleshas. The *künjung of kleshas* brings about internal suffering through the arising of conflicting emotions.

künjung of karma. *See* künjung.

künjung of kleshas. *See* künjung.

lam (Tib.: lam; Skt.: marga). Path.

le kyi tha (Tib.: las kyi mtha'). End of karma. *See* eightfold path, noble.

mahayana (Skt.). Great vehicle. The stage of Buddha's teaching that emphasizes the union of wisdom and compassion. It is the path of the bodhisattva, one whose life is dedicated to helping others on the path to liberation.

mi-lop-lam (Tib.: mi slobs lam). Path of no more learning. *See* paths, five.

naga (Skt.). Snake. A class of deities with human torsos and serpent-like lower bodies, said to inhabit low-lying marshy areas and bodies of water. Trungpa Rinpoche likened the modern equivalent of being born into a family of nagas as being born into a family of Mafiosi.

neuroses. Kleshas. Chögyam Trungpa Rinpoche tended to use psychological terminology rather than more religious or philosophical language in translating key dharmic terms. *See* note 1 for Chapter 1 on page 127.

ngak (Tib.: ngag). Speech. *See* eightfold path, noble.

ngejung (Tib.: nges 'byung). Real becoming. First of two types of renunciation: disgust with samsara.

ngepar shepa (Tib.: nges par shes pa). Real conviction.

nidanas, twelve (Skt.). Chain of causation. The twelve links in the chain of causation of interdependent origination: ignorance, formation, consciousness, name and form, six senses, contact, feeling, craving, clinging, becoming, birth, and death. The web of mutually conditioned psychological and physical phenomena that constitute individual existence, and entangle sentient beings in samsara.

nihilism. *See* eternalism/nihilism.

nirmanakaya (Skt.). *See* kayas, three.

nirodha (Skt.). (Tib.: gokpa; 'gog pa). Cessation. Also, the state of enlightenment or freedom.

nirvana (Skt.). Extinguished. The Tibetan translation of this word, *nya-ngen ledepa* (mya ngan las 'das pa) means "gone beyond suffering," a state of no more suffering achieved when one is completely enlightened; used in contrast to samsara.

nonreturner. A practitioner who, through diligent practice, is not reborn into samsara.

nontheism. A doctrine of neither believing in nor relying on an external god or savior.

nyönmong (Tib.: nyon mongs; Skt.: klesha). *See* klesha.

nyönmong künjung (Tib.: nyon mongs kun 'byung). Origin of all the defilements; or where all the defilements and pain are created.

nyönmong kyi drippa (Tib.: nyon mongs kyi sgrib pa). The obscuration of negative emotions brought about from pakchak kyi drippa (flickering thoughts).

once-returner. A practitioner who, due to remaining karmic debt, returns for one more lifetime to samsara.

oryoki (Jap.). A formal style of serving and eating food in a shrine room that has its origins in Zen Buddhism.

pakchak kyi drippa (Tib.: bag chags kyi sgrib pa). The obscuration of habitual tendencies. Flickering thoughts.

paramita (Skt.). Perfection. Transcendent virtue; literally, "going across" (from the shore of samsara to the other shore, nirvana). The bodhisattva cultivates the six transcendent virtues of generosity, discipline, patience, exertion, meditation, and prajna (knowledge).

paths, five. Five stages of the path to enlightenment as enumerated by Atisha Dipankara, Gampopa, and others: (1) tsog-lam (Tib.: tshogs lam), the path of accumulation; (2) jor-lam (sbyor lam), the path of unification; (3) thong-lam (mthong lam), the path of seeing; (4) gom-lam (sgom lam), the path of meditation; and (5) mi-lop-lam (mi slobs lam), the path of no-more-learning.

prajna (Skt.). Knowledge. Prajna can refer to perfect knowledge, or transcendent wisdom, or to ordinary intellectual understanding. Ordinary prajna is understanding the world and how things work on a mundane level. Dharmic prajna encompasses a direct experience of the mind and its processes; and, in later stages of the path, penetrating insight that discovers both the world and the self to be illusory.

pratimoksha (Skt.). Buddhist vows of personal liberation; monastic and lay precepts.

ri-me (Tib.: ris med). Unbiased. The eighteenth-century nonsectarian movement that consolidated the contemplative traditions and schools of Tibet, emphasizing meditation and retreat practice as foundations of the spiritual life.

saddharma (Skt.). True law. Excellent or true dharma.

samadhi (Skt.). (Tib.: tingdzin). Meditation, mental stillness. (1) One-pointedness; one of the seven limbs of enlightenment. (2) A state of consciousness where mental activity ceases; total absorption in the object of meditation.

samsara (Skt.). (Tib: khorwa). Cyclic existence; the continual repetitive cycle of birth, death, and bardo that arises from ordinary beings' grasping and fixating on a self and experiences. All states of consciousness in the six realms (see note 2 for Chapter 1 on page 127), including the god realms, characterized by pleasure and power, are bound by this process. Samsara arises out of ignorance and is characterized by suffering.

samskara (Skt.) Mental formation. The second nidana, pictured as a potter's wheel, representing conceptual mind forming itself into a certain shape.

samudaya (Skt.). (Tib.: künjung). *See* künjung.

sang-gye (Tib.: sangs rgyas; Skt.: buddha). Buddha, or awake. *See* buddha.

sangha (Skt.). Community. The third of the three jewels of refuge. In the hinayana, sangha refers specifically to Buddhist monks and nuns. In the mahayana, the mahasangha also includes lay practitioners. As an object of refuge, "noble sangha" may refer to the assembly of bodhisattvas and arhats, those who have attained realization.

semjung (Tib.: sems byung). The fifty-one mental events arising from the mind. Flickering thoughts that trigger the skandhas and kleshas.

shamatha (Skt.). (Tib.: shi-ne; zhi gnas). Peaceful abiding. Mindfulness practice. The meditation practice of taming and stabilizing the mind.

shamatha-vipashyana (Skt.). The practice or state of meditation in which the stability of shamatha and the insight of vipashyana are unified.

sherap (Tib.: shes rab; Skt.: prajna). Knowledge. *See* prajna.

shila (Skt.). Discipline. Dharmic training is based on a combination of shila (discipline), samadhi (meditation), and prajna (knowledge).

shinjang (Tib.: shin sbyangs). Thoroughly processed or trained through meditation practice; one of the seven limbs of enlightenment. Refers to the flexibility and serviceability of the mind to focus on whatever object of meditation is desired. It is an overall state of well-being and ease, and is the result of shamatha and vipashyana practice.

shunyata (Skt.). Emptiness. A completely open and unbounded clarity of mind characterized by groundlessness and freedom from all conceptual frameworks. Shunyata is inseparable from awakened qualities such as compassion. It could be called "openness," since "emptiness" can convey the mistaken notion of a state of voidness or blankness. In fact, shunyata is inseparable from compassion and all other awakened qualities.

siddha (Skt.). A term for an enlightened master in the tantric tradition. One who has acquired extraordinary powers and is capable of working miracles.

skandhas (Skt.). Heaps or baskets. The self is not one solid independent thing, but a composite of five skandhas, or aggregates: form, feeling, perception-impulse, concept, and consciousness.

spiritual materialism. The use of a spiritual path or discipline to support and solidify self-interest, a basic misunderstanding of the purpose of a spiritual path.

stream-winner. A student who has entered the hinayana path.

sutra (Skt.). Juncture. Hinayana and mahayana texts in the Buddhist canon that are attributed to Shakyamuni Buddha. Literally, "meeting point" or "junction," referring to the meeting of the Buddha's enlightenment and the student's understanding. A sutra is usually a dialogue between the Buddha and one or more of his disciples elaborating a particular topic of dharma.

tang-nyom (Tib.: btang snyoms). Equilibrium or equanimity. One of the seven limbs of enlightenment.

tantra (Tib.: gyü, rgyud). Literally, "continuity." The vajrayana teachings. *See* vajrayana.

tathagatagarbha (Skt.). Buddha nature; the intrinsic state of wakefulness inherent in all beings.

tawa (Tib.: lta ba). View. *See* eightfold path, noble.

tepa (Tib.: dad pa). Faith. Described in this book as feeling steady and confident in the path, and knowing what to cultivate and what to avoid.

tharpa (Tib.: thar pa; Skt.: moksha). Liberation.

theism. The belief in an external deity or savior.

thong-lam (Tib.). Path of seeing. *See* paths, five.

timuk (Tib.: gti mug; Skt.: moha). The klesha of ignorance or bewilderment. For fundamental ignorance, *see* avidya.

tingdzin (Tib.). (Skt.: samadhi: ting 'dzin). Meditation. In this volume, described as one-pointed, focused, and accurate mind. *See* eightfold path, noble

tokpa (Tib.: rtog pa). Understanding. *See* eightfold path, noble.

töndam (Tib.: don dam). Absolute truth; ultimate nature; superior understanding.

trenpa (Tib.:dran pa.). Recollection. One of the seven limbs of enlightenment. *See* eightfold path, noble.

tsog-lam (Tib.: tshogs lam). Path of accumulation. *See* paths, five.

tsölwa (Tib.: rtsol wa). Effort. *See* eightfold path, noble.

tsöndrü (Tib.: brtson 'grus). Exertion; one of the seven limbs of enlightenment. Described in this volume as tremendous effort that is applied to practice, with a sense of delight and appreciation. *See* eightfold path, noble.

tsowa (Tib.: 'tsho ba). Livelihood. *See* eightfold path, noble.

tülku (Tib.: sprul sku). "Emanation body." A term used for a person who is recognized as the reincarnation of a previously deceased enlightened being. (for further reading, *see* Appendix I in *Born in Tibet* (Boston: Shambhala Publications, 2000).

two-fold ego. (1) Ego of self; (2) Ego of dharmas. Ego of self is the attachment to the idea of an independently existing self. Ego of dharmas is the attachment to the idea of an independently existing other, or the phenomenal world. The two mutually reinforce one another, and perpetuate a sense of duality.

vajrayana (Skt.). Diamond, or indestructible, vehicle. The third of the three main paths of Tibetan Buddhism. Vajrayana is also known as the sudden path, because its practices lead one to realize enlightenment in one lifetime.

Vidyadhara, the (Skt.). Wisdom holder. An epithet of Chögyam Trungpa Rinpoche. In his early years of teaching in North America, Trungpa Rinpoche was simply referred to as *Rinpoche*, or "precious one." Then he was referred to as *the Vajracharya,* or "holder of the vajra" (vajrayana teachings). Later he became known as *the Vidyadhara,* or "wisdom holder."

vipashyana (Skt.). (Tib.: lhakthong; lhag mthong). Awareness. In Tibetan, "clear seeing." Insight arising from direct meditative experience or contemplative analysis. An open, expansive quality of meditative practice complementary to the stability and groundedness of shamatha.

yana (Skt.). (Tib: thekpa; theg pa). Literally, "vehicle." A means of traveling on the path. A stage of the path, such as hinayana or mahayana.

yangdak (Tib.: yang dag). Perfect. *See* eightfold path, noble.

TEXT SOURCES

This book is based on Vajradhatu Seminary talks given by Chögyam Trungpa Rinpoche between 1973 and 1986, during the hinayana portion of the Seminary. Trungpa Rinpoche went through the logic of the four truths four times, in 1974, 1975, 1978, and 1983. Each time he covered this topic, he emphasized different points of the teaching. The book also includes material from the 1980 talk "Basic Anxiety," in which Trungpa Rinpoche further explicated the way in which a practitioner recognizes the reality of suffering and the significance of the first noble truth, and the 1980 talk "Introduction to Practice," in which he presents a pithy summary of the four noble truths. Below is a list of sources for each chapter of the book.

Introduction: 1980 Talk 1, "Introduction to Practice"

The First Noble Truth

    Chapter 1. Recognizing the Reality of Suffering: 1980 Talk 2 "Basic Anxiety"; 1983 Talk 4 "Suffering"

    Chapter 2. Dissecting the Experience of Suffering: 1975 Talk 5, "Sravakayana"; 1978 Talk 5 "Suffering"

The Second Noble Truth

    Chapter 3. The Power of Flickering Thoughts: 1974 Talk 9, "Awareness and Suffering"; 1975 Talk 6, "The Origin of Suffering"; 1983 Talk 5, "The Origin of Suffering"

    Chapter 4. The Development of Set Patterns: 1974 Talk 10 "The Origin of Suffering"

    Chapter 5. Perpetually Re-creating Suffering: 1978 Talk 6, "Origin of Suffering"; 1978 Talk 7, "The Origin of Suffering II: Steady Course"

The Third Noble Truth

Chapter 6. Awakening and Blossoming: 1974 Talk 11, "The Cessation of Suffering"

Chapter 7. Meditation and the Path to Buddhahood: 1983 Talk 6, "Cessation and Path"

Chapter 8. Transcending Samsara and Nirvana: 1975 Talk 7, "Cessation"; 1978 Talk 8, "Cessation"

The Fourth Noble Truth

Chapter 9. The Doubtless Path: 1975 Talk 8, "The Path"

Chapter 10. The Five Paths: 1973 Talk 13, "Middle Level of the Path of Accumulation"; 1974 Talk 12, "The Path"; 1978 Talk 9, "The Path"

The editor gratefully acknowledges the use or adaptation of glossary entries from the following sources: *Illusion's Game* by Chögyam Trungpa, in *The Collected Works of Chögyam Trungpa,* vol. 5 (Boston: Shambhala Publications, 2004). *The Chariot of Liberation* by Ösel Tendzin and Dorje Löppon Lodrö Dorje (Halifax: Vajradhatu Publications, 2002). Used by permission of Lodrö Dorje. *The Three Vehicles of Buddhist Practice* by Khenchen Thrangu Rinpoche, translated by Ken Holmes and edited by Clark Johnson (Boulder: Namo Buddha Seminar, 1998). Used by permission. *The Rain of Wisdom,* translated by the Nālandā Translation Committee under the direction of Chögyam Trungpa (Boston: Shambhala Publications, 1989). Used by permission of the Nālandā Translation Committee. *Glimpses of Mahayana* by Chögyam Trungpa (Halifax: Vajradhatu Publications, 2001).

"The First Turning of the Wheel of Dharma" is reprinted from *Old Path White Clouds: Walking in the Footsteps of the Buddha* by Thich Nhat Hanh (Berkeley, Calif.: Parallax Press, 1991). Reprinted with permission. www.parallax.org.

The essay "The Practice of Meditation: Basic Instructions and Guidelines" is reprinted from an unpublished article by Chögyam Trungpa Rinpoche.

RESOURCES

For information about meditation instruction or to find a practice
center near you, please contact one of the following:

Shambhala International
1084 Tower Road
Halifax, Nova Scotia
Canada B3H 2Y5
Phone: (902) 425-4275
Web site: www.shambhala.org

Karmê Chöling
369 Patneaude Lane
Barnet, Vermont 05821
Phone: (802) 633-2384
Web site: www.karmecholing.org

Shambhala Mountain Center
4921 Country Road 68C
Red Feather Lakes, Colorado 80545
Phone: (970) 881-2184
Web site: www.shambhalamountain.org

Gampo Abbey
Pleasant Bay, Nova Scotia
Canada B0E 2P0
Phone: (902) 224-2752
Web site: www.gampoabbey.org

Dechen Choling
Mas Marvent
87700 St. Yrieix Aixe
France
Phone: +33 5-55-03-55-52
Web site: www.dechencholing.org

Naropa University is the only accredited, Buddhist-inspired university in North America. For more information, contact:

Naropa University
2130 Arapahoe Avenue
Boulder, Colorado 80302
Phone: (303) 444-0202
Web site: www.naropa.edu

Ocean of Dharma Quotes of the Week brings you the teachings of Chögyam Trungpa Rinpoche. An e-mail is sent out several times each week containing a quote from Chögyam Trungpa's extensive teachings. Quotations of material may be from unpublished material, forthcoming publications, or previously published sources. Ocean of Dharma Quotes of the Week are selected by Carolyn Rose Gimian. To enroll go to OceanofDharma.com.

For information regarding meditation instruction, please visit the website of Shambhala International at www.shambhala.org. This website contains information about the more than a hundred centers affiliated with Shambhala.

The Chögyam Trungpa Legacy Project was established to help preserve, disseminate, and expand Chögyam Trungpa's legacy. The Legacy Project supports the preservation, propagation, and publication of Trungpa Rinpoche's dharma teachings. This includes plans for the creation of a comprehensive virtual archive and learning community. For information, go to ChogyamTrungpa.com

For publications from Vajradhatu Publications and Kalapa Recordings, including both books and audiovisual materials, go to www.shambhalashop.com

For information about the archive of the author's work, please contact the Shambhala Archives: archives@shambhala.org.

INDEX

abhidharma, 28, 36
absentmindedness, 33
absolute truth (Tib.: *töndam*),
    102–3, 125
absorption, meditative, 77, 82, 83,
    98, 122, 128n2
    See also samadhi
accumulation, path of, 99–103,
    124–25
aging, 18–19
    See also old age
aggression, 2–3
    set pattern of, 39, 42, 120
    thoughts of, 52–53
    unmeritorious karma and, 50
all-pervasive suffering, 24–26, 26,
    27, 120
anger, xv
    root klesha of, 47, 55, 120
    unmeritorious karma and, 50
animal realm, 84
anxiety, xv
    basic, 1–2, 7, 9–10
    overcoming, 4
    recognizing, 7, 8
    yearning to cure, 8
anxiousness, 2–3
ape instinct, 15, 33, 34
    See also habitual patterns
appreciation, 104
arhats, 82, 83, 113

attachment, xv, 102
attention, shifts of, 36–37
awakening, 13, 64–65
    See also enlightenment;
        liberation
awareness, 117
    cessation and, 66–67
    loss of, 33
    suffering and, 34
    two extremes and, 42

basic goodness, 7, 35
basic sanity, 78, 79, 94, 95, 124
    See also sanity
bewilderment, 34
    root kleshas and, 47, 48
    samsara, as seed of, 65, 122
    See also ignorance; stupidity
birth, xv, 16–17, 22, 26, 27–29, 119
birth and death, period between,
    16, 22–24, 119
bodhi, seven limbs of, 106–7, 125
bodhisattva path, 103
bodhisattvas, 82
body
    caring for, 72–73
    in meditation practice, 117–18
    suffering of, 27–29
    and suffering of death, 21
    unmeritorious karma of,
        50–51, 120–21

boredom, 25
brahmahood, 84, 128–29n5
breath, meditation instructions for,
    118
buddha, 82
    meanings of, 64, 65
    in the palm of your hand, 11
buddha nature, 77, 94
Buddha (Shakyamuni), 3–4, 64
    authority of, 14
    first sermon of, xv–xvi, 67
    liberation of, 69–70, 71
    worldly norms of, 29
buddhadharma, path of, 11–12
    See also Buddhism; dharma
buddhahood, 66–67, 70
Buddhism, 7, 8, 111–15
    freestyle, 49
    nontheism of, 13
    and other paths,
        differentiated, 98
    pain in, 28, 29
    peace in, 86
    satisfaction in, 25
    three yanas of, 9, 12
    Zen, 72

centering, 92
cessation (third noble truth), 27,
    75, 86
    achieving, 86–87
    candle analogy, 69
    degrees of, 76
    experience of, 63–64, 67
    foundation for, 50
    hinayana, view of, 70, 71, 73,
        82–83, 85
    and path, 70
    possibility of, 4, 64, 66, 69

samsara and, 14, 66
striving for, 71
    See also twelve aspects of
        cessation
change, suffering of, 26–27, 120, 127n1
Christianity, 84
clarity, 71, 81, 124
    See also insight
clear seeing, path of, 82
clinging, xv
    See also attachment
cocoon, 35
comfort, 71
common path, 97–98, 99
concentration, xvi, 98, 114
    See also samadhi
concept, skandha of, 39
confidence, 76, 104, 113
confusion
    cutting the root, 102
    at death, 22
    kleshas and, 46–47
    and pain, experience of, 28, 33
    recognizing, 7, 8
consciousness, skandha of, 39
contentment (Tib.: chok-she), 99, 103
conviction (Tib.: ngepar shepa),
    100–102

daily life (everyday life, ordinary
    life)
    karma and, 48–49
    meditation in, 118
    path and, 94, 95
    samsara and, 9–10
death, xv
    eternalism and, 45
    suffering of, 16, 20–22, 26,
        27–29, 119, 120

deception, 3, 4
Deer Park, xv
delightfulness, 104
desire, xv, 35, 47, 120
    See also passion
dharma, 43, 73
    disparaging, 53
    karmic consequence of
        practicing, 56, 122
    as medicine, 114–15
    nature of, 112–15
    orientation of, 99
    profundity of, 79–80
    wheel, first turning of, xv–xvi
    See also path (fourth noble
        truth); spiritual path
dharmas, separating, 106, 125, 129n3
dignity
    cessation, token of, 80–81
    development of, 72
    disbelief in, 53
    selflessness and, 93
discipline, 72–73, 79
discomfort, 20, 49
dissatisfaction, 24, 33
divine achievement, 83
doubt
    necessity of, 96
    on path of meditation, 109
    root klesha of, 47–48, 120
dream state, 65
duality, 108
duhkha. See suffering (first noble
    truth)

eating properly, 72, 122
effort
    cessation and, 69, 70

perfect (eightfold path limb),
    108, 111, 125
ego
    cessation and, 87
    eternalism and, 45
    four noble truths and, 13
    pain of, 34
    as sense of center, 92–93, 96
    two extremes and, 42
    twofold, 111, 114, 129n5
egolessness, 91, 92, 123
eight types of suffering, 16–26, 119
    all-pervasive suffering, 24–26,
        26, 27, 120
    birth, 16–17
    coming across what is not
        desirable, 23, 26, 119, 120
    death, 20–22
    not getting what you want,
        23–24, 26–27, 119, 120
    not holding on to what is
        desirable, 23, 26–27, 119, 120
    old age, 18–19
    sickness, 19–20
eightfold path, xv–xvi, 108–11, 125
emotions, 36–37
    See also kleshas
emptiness (Skt. *shunyata*), 40–41, 91,
    92, 123
energy, 86, 111
enlightenment, 71, 75–76, 108,
    111, 112
    seven limbs of, 106–7, 125
    See also awakening; liberation
entertainment
    ego fixation and, 27
    kleshas and, 46–47
    old age and, 18–19
environment, caring for, 73

envy, 52
equilibrium (Tib.: *tang-nyom*), 107, 125
eternalism, 39, 40, 41–42, 45, 120
    overcoming, 92, 96, 123
everyday life. *See* daily life (everyday life, ordinary life)
evil acts, ten, 50–53
exertion, 33, 114
    on path of seeing, 106, 125
    on path of unification, 103, 104, 125
extremes, two, 40–42

faith, 103–4, 125
fear, xv, 45, 72
fearlessness, 52
feeling, skandha of, 39
first noble truth. *See* suffering
five aggregates. *See* skandhas, five
five paths, 82, 99, 111–12, 114, 124–25, 128n1, 129n1
    accumulation, path of, 99–103, 124–25
    meditation, path of, 108–11, 125
    no more learning, path of, 82, 108, 111, 125, 128n1
    prajna and, 105, 106, 129n3
    seeing, path of, 105–7, 108, 109, 125
    unification, path of, 103–5, 125
fixation
    all-pervasive suffering and, 26
    origin of suffering and, 46
    samsara, cause of, 65–66, 122
form, skandha of, 39
formless god realm, 84
four noble truths, xv, 64, 67, 114
    divisions of, 13–14

sixteen incantations of, 100–102, 124, 129n2
    See also suffering (first noble truth); origin of suffering (second noble truth); cessation (third noble truth); path (fourth noble truth)
four qualities of the path, 93–96
four ways of developing wholesomeness, 72–73, 122
fourth noble truth. *See* path
freedom, 73, 84
    See also enlightenment
fruition, 95–96, 124

gap, 56
general path. *See* common path
generosity, 53, 121
gentleness, 53, 121
genuineness, 76
God, 8
god realm, 84, 98
Godhead, 84, 128–29n5
gokpa (Tib.). *See* cessation; enlightenment
goodness
    on Buddhist path, 99
    partial, 58
    See also basic goodness
gossip, 51–52, 121
grasping. *See* fixation
Great Eastern Sun vision, 52
groundlessness, 87

habitual patterns
    of avoidance, 49
    of ego, 13, 39
        (*See also* skandhas, five)
    at fruition, 95–96

obscuration of, 36
on path of meditation, 110
sickness as, 20
of suffering, 14–15
See also seven ego-oriented
patterns (set patterns)
happiness, 113
maintaining, 1–2
myth of, 27
harm, hoping to create, 52–53, 121
hell realm, 84
helplessness, 20
hinayana, 7
attention in, 37
cessation/liberation in, 70, 71, 73,
82–83, 85
consciousness in, 41
nirvana in, 95–96
other yanas, relationship to,
11–12, 85, 115
samsara, approach to, 58–59, 101
suffering and, 9, 10
Hinduism, 41, 83, 84, 128–29n5
hope, 8, 71, 86
hopelessness, 49
human realm, 84
humanness, 1
humor, 10, 14–15, 86
hungry ghost realm, 84

ignorance, xv, 59, 114
cocoon of, 35
fundamental (Skt.: *avidya*),
48, 108
klesha of (Tib.: *timuk*), 47, 48,
120
on path of meditation, 110
set pattern of, 39, 42, 120
suffering and, 33

impermanence
of four noble truths, 101
overcoming, 91, 92
protecting oneself from, 39,
40, 120
of time and space, 102
incantations, sixteen, 100–102, 129n2
individual salvation, 11, 70–71, 73
inherited suffering, 16–22, 119
insight, 15, 94, 124
intellect, 81
on path of seeing, 106
on path of unification, 103, 105,
125
intention, 57–58, 122
intrigue, 51, 121
irritation, 33–34

jealous-god realm, 84
jealousy, xv, 52
jhana states, 82, 83, 128n2
See also absorption,
meditative
joy, xv, xvi, 114
all-pervasive suffering and, 24,
25
on the path of seeing, 106–7, 125

karma, 46, 120–22, 128n3
consequences of, 48, 54–59, 110,
121–22
meritorious, 53–54, 58, 121
origin of suffering and, 46,
48–50
on the path of meditation, 108
perfect end of (eightfold path
limb), 108, 110, 125
preventing, 76
seeds of, 15

shared, 56–57, 122
suffering and, 15, 16
transforming, 56, 59, 128n4
unmeritorious, 50–53, 58, 120–21
killing (taking life), 50, 51, 121
kleshas (Skt.), 7–8, 127n1
cessation and, 77, 78, 80
development of, 45–46, 47
origin of, 35–37
patterns of, 2–3
six root, 46–48, 58, 120, 127–28n2
(*See also* individual kleshas)
See also neurosis
Kongtrül, Jamgön, 28
künjung (Tib.). *See* origin of suffering
(second noble truth)

laziness, freedom from, 107
liberation
glimpses of, 63–64
individual, 11, 70–71, 73
styles of, 69–70
See also enlightenment
livelihood, perfect (eightfold path
limb), 108, 110–11, 125
lust, 3, 35, 42, 47, 54
See also passion
lying, 51, 121

mahayana path, 11–12, 77, 85, 111
mantra of experience, 100–102, 124,
129n2
meditation
as cure, 114–15
inspiration for, 79
instructions for, 117–18
karma during, 46

in nontheistic tradition, 108
perfect (eightfold path limb),
108, 111, 125
psychological development
through, 111–12
result of (Tib.: *shinjang*), 70–72
second noble truth and, 37
simplicity and, 78
and suffering, role in
understanding, 34
two extremes and, 41
wholesomeness and, 73, 122
See also one-pointedness;
shamatha; sitting
meditation practice
meditation, path of, 108–11, 125
memory, 104–5
merit, 100
meritorious deeds, ten, 53–54
meticulousness, 72, 73, 122
mind
and body, 106–7
on Buddhist path, 98
cessation and, 78
on path of accumulation, 100
unmeritorious karma of, 52–53,
121
mindfulness, xvi, 117
cessation and, 66–67
reminders of, 72
See also one-pointedness;
shamatha
miracles, 83
misery, general, 16, 24–26, 119, 120

Nagarjuna, 83, 128n3 (chap. 8)
national karma, 57
negative words, 51, 121

neurosis, 2, 112, 127n1
    all-pervasive suffering and, 24
    cessation and, 78, 123
    overcoming, 4
    and real pain, 28
    transcending, 94
    wearing out, 86
    See also anxiety; kleshas
nidanas, 36, 48, 108, 110
nihilism, 39, 40–41, 42, 120
nirmanakaya, 29
nirodha (Skt.). See cessation (third
    noble truth)
nirvana
    hassles of, overcoming, 84–85
    permanent, 95–96, 124
    possibility of, 67
    samsara and, 14
    sign of, 80
    See also cessation (third
        noble truth)
no more learning, path of, 82, 108,
    111, 125, 128n1
Noble Eightfold Path. See eightfold
    path
"noble prajna," 81
nonexistence, 28
nonreturners, 82, 83
nontheism, 45, 92
"nouveau-riche samsara," 9
nyönmong (Tib.). See klesha

obscuration, 36
obstacles
    to cessation, 63, 78, 82
    of ego, 13
    of karmic consequences, 54
    to the path, 67, 93

    of pleasure, searching for, 92
    of samsara, 64–65
old age, xv, 16, 18–19, 22, 26, 119
once-returners, 82
one-pointedness, 103, 105, 107, 111, 125
openness, 53
opinion, root klesha of, 47, 48, 120
ordinary life. See daily life (everyday
    life, ordinary life)
origin of suffering (second noble
    truth), 34–35, 45, 46, 120–22
    awareness and, 39
    cessation and, 76–77
    contemplating, 43
    karma and, 48–54, 58–59
    klesha and, 46–48, 58–59
    prajna, role in overcoming, 81
    progress of, 36–37
    and samsara, relationship to, 14
original sin, 27
oryoki practice, 72

pain
    overcoming, 29
    pleasure and, 10
    recognizing, 10
    as reference point, 8–9
    tendency toward, 35–36
    understanding, 8, 28
    See also suffering (first noble
        truth)
passion, 2–3, 35, 59
    examining, 102
    realm of, 82–83
    root klesha of, 48
    set pattern of, 39, 42, 120
    sexual misconduct and, 50, 51
    See also desire

passionlessness, 86, 123
path (fourth noble truth), 123–25
  Buddhist and common
    differentiated, 98
  cessation and, 70
  doubtlessness of, 96
  four qualities of, 93–96, 123–24
  logic of, 113–15
  misunderstanding, 97
  nature of, 91, 93, 96
  obstacles to, 67
  sequence of, 91–93, 98, 123
  See also five paths; spiritual path
peace, xv, xvi
  complete, 86
  development of, 72
  See also nirvana
perception
  mistaken, 47
  sense, 18, 19, 105
perception-impulse, skandha of, 39
Ping-Pong ball (of fixation), 65–66
pleasure, 10, 20
  all-pervasive suffering and, 24,
    25
  overcoming search for, 92, 96,
    123
  pain of, 8–9, 27–28
poverty mentality, 52
prajna (Skt.), 81, 83, 114
  See also intellect
pratimoksha (Skt.). See individual
    salvation
pride, 2–3
  in cessation, 79
  root klesha of, 47, 120
profundity, 78–80, 123
purification, complete, 86, 123

realization, xvi
  perfect (eightfold path limb)
    (See understanding, perfect)
realms of existence, 8–9, 84, 127n2
rebirth
  karmic consequence of, 54–55
recollection
  on path of seeing, 106, 125
  on path of unification, 103,
    104–5, 125
  perfect (eightfold path limb),
    108, 111, 125
relative truth (Tib.: kündzop),
    102, 103, 125
renunciation, 85, 98, 103, 123
  in cutting karma, 110
  types of, 99
respect for life, 53, 121
resting, 72, 122

sacredness, 53, 54, 121
saddharma (Skt.), 114–15
sadness, xv
salvation, 40
  individual, 11, 70–71, 73
  levels of, 82–83
samadhi (Skt.)
  on path of meditation, 111
  on path of seeing, 105, 106, 107, 125
  views of, 98
  See also one-pointedness
samsara, 35, 51, 64–65
  four noble truths and, 13–14
  generating, 3
  hinayana approach to, 58–59
  and nirvana, transcending, 85, 87
  nostalgia for, 104–5
  nouveau riche, 9

origin of suffering and, 45–46

pervasiveness of, 8–10, 12

three categories of, 65–66, 122

understanding, 11

samskara (Skt.), 108, 110

sanity

cessation and, 69, 81, 84

developing, 75

and pain, effect on, 28

on the path, 99, 103, 127n1

See also basic sanity

Sarnath, India, xv, 67

satisfaction, 25, 103

second noble truth. *See* origin of suffering

seeing, path of, 105–7, 108, 109, 125

self, notion of, 15

in death, 21–22

examining, 13

See also ego

self-discipline, 70, 80–81

sense perceptions

appreciating, 105

old age and, 18, 19

separation, pain of, 21

seven ego-oriented patterns (set patterns), 39–42, 120

seven limbs of enlightenment, 106–7, 125

sexual behavior

misconduct, 50, 51, 121

wholesomeness, 53, 121

shamatha (Skt.), 11, 12, 72, 114

cessation and, 77, 78

discipline of, 94, 100, 102

karma during, 76

on path of accumulation, 100, 102

on path of seeing, 107

on path of unification, 104

prajna, developing in, 81

shamatha-vipashyana, 71

shinjang (Tib.)

developing, 70–72

on the path of seeing, 107

sickness, xv, 16, 19–20, 22, 26, 27–29, 119

simplicity

cessation, aspect of, 71, 78, 123

cultivating, 78

meritorious karma, type of, 53, 121

on the path of accumulation, 100, 102, 103

sitting meditation practice

anxiety and, 9, 11

discipline, role in, 73

karma, effect on, 56

path, role in, 94–95

posture in, 117–18

See also meditation; *shamatha*

six realms of existence, 8–9, 84, 127n2

six root kleshas, 46–48, 58, 120, 127–28n2

See also individual klesha

six types of karmic consequences, 54–59, 121–22

skandhas, five, xv, 15

all-pervasive suffering and, 27

origin of, 36

self, regarding as, 39, 120

sleep, 65, 122

sloppiness, 72

speech

meritorious, 53, 121

perfect (eightfold path limb), 108, 109, 110, 125

unmeritorious, 51–52, 121

spiritual master, 40, 83–84, 109
spiritual materialism, 40, 66–67, 92
spiritual path, 27, 127n1
   common, 97–98
   exertion on, 33
   qualities and consequences,
      13–14
   See also path (fourth noble
      truth)
spirituality, 24
stealing, 50, 51, 121
straightforwardness, 53, 121
stream-winners, 82
stupidity, 10, 35
   first noble truth and, 33
   root kleshas and, 47, 48
suchness, 94, 104, 108, 123
suffering (first noble truth), xv, 8,
      9, 49, 119
   cure for, 114–15
   definitions of, 14
   as ground, 97
   immunity to, 25–26
   necessity of understanding,
      14–15
   overcoming, 81, 91, 92
   recognizing, 7–12
   and samsara, 14, 66–67, 122
   of suffering, 26, 119
   three patterns of, 26–29, 119
   understanding, 34
   See also eight types of
      suffering

taking life, 50, 51, 121
teacher. See spiritual master
ten evil acts, 50–53
theism, 45, 84
third noble truth. See cessation

thoughts
   all-pervasive suffering and,
      24–25
   cessation and, 77
   discursive, 52
   karma and, 15, 16
   in meditation practice, 118
   on path of accumulation, 100,
      102
   and second noble truth, 34,
      36–37
   three categories of samsara, 65–66,
      122
three jewels, 56, 122
three patterns of suffering, 26–29, 119
training, 70, 108, 125
   See also meditation; path;
      shinjang
tranquility, samsaric, 47
transparency, 77, 102
Treasury of Knowledge (Kongtrül),
      77, 85
Trungpa, Chögyam, 73, 127n1, 128n4
truth, twofold, 102–3, 124–25
truthfulness, 53, 121
twelve aspects of cessation, 77, 122–23
   adorned, 83–84
   beyond calculation, 85–86
   completion, signs of, 82–83
   especially supreme, 85, 87
   incompletion, 81–82
   nature, 77–78
   omission, with, 84
   omission, without, 84–85
   profundity, 78–80
   sign, 80–81
   ultimate, 81
   without ornament, 83
twelve nidanas, 36, 48, 108, 110

understanding, perfect (eightfold
    path limb), 108, 109, 110, 125
unification, path of, 103–5, 125

vajrayana, 11, 12, 70, 82, 115, 128n1
Varanasi, India, xv
view, 39, 40, 120
    klesha of, 48
    perfect (eightfold path limb),
        108, 109, 110, 125
vipashyana, 102
virtue, appreciating, 56, 122

volitional action, 48–49, 54–55, 110,
    121
    See also karma

wakefulness, 11, 52
white karmic consequences, 56, 57,
    58, 122
wholesomeness, 7, 72–73, 122
wisdom, good, 53, 121
wishful thinking, 52

Zen Buddhism, 72